DEVON AND CORNWALL RECORD SOCIETY

New Series, Volume 55

DEVON AND CORNWALL RECORD SOCIETY

New Series, Volume 55

The Chancery Case Between Nicholas Radford and
Thomas Tremayne: the Exeter Depositions of 1439

Edited by Hannes Kleineke

Exeter
2013

ISBN 978 0 901853 55 4

Designed and typeset by Kestrel Data, Exeter

Printed and bound in Great Britain by
Short Run Press, Exeter

CONTENTS

ACKNOWLEDGEMENTS

The principal document edited in this volume was originally discovered and brought to my attention by Dr. David Grummitt in the course of cataloguing work on the PRO class C4. I subsequently lost sight of it, but at a later date I came across it independently during my own researches in that class. Dr. Grummitt and I had originally intended to produce a joint edition of the manuscript, which was prevented by other commitments, and I am most grateful to Dr. Grummitt for his agreement that I should go ahead and produce this edition on my own.

In the course of my work on the manuscript, I have incurred a number of debts. I am grateful to Exeter City Council for permission to use the cover image. The map of Exeter is reproduced with the kind permission of Devon Heritage Services. Professor Nicholas Orme generously shared with me information on the clergy mentioned in the document. Dr. Simon Payling read and commented upon a draft of the introduction to this volume. At various times I have discussed aspects of the manuscript with friends and colleagues, among them Jim Bolton, Linda Clark, Justin Colson, Michael Hicks, Nick Kingwell, Carole Rawcliffe, and James Ross. Papers based on the introduction have been presented to the Late Medieval Seminar at the Institute of Historical Research in London, and the Fifteenth-Century Conference 2009 held at the university of St. Andrews. I am grateful to the members of both audiences for their comments. Work done for my employer, the History of Parliament Trust, has informed parts of the introduction and some of the biographies provided in the appendix. I am grateful to the trustees for permission to draw upon it. Much of the background research for this volume was conducted in the Public Record Office, Kew, and the Devon Record Office, Exeter. I am grateful to the staff of both repositories for their kindness and patience. Any errors that remain are, naturally, my own. Finally, I am indebted to Professor Andrew Thorpe, the Devon and Cornwall Record Society's Honorary Editor, for his efforts in seeing this volume through to publication.

H.K.

London, January 2012

LISTS OF ILLUSTRATIONS

LIST OF ABBREVIATIONS

Add.	Additional
BL	British Library, London
CCR	*Calendar of the Close Rolls*
CFR	*Calendar of the Fine Rolls*
CIPM	*Calendar of Inquisitions post Mortem*
CP	*Complete Peerage*
CPL	*Calendar of Papal Letters*
CPR	*Calendar of the Patent Rolls*
EHR	*English Historical Review*
MS	Manuscript
PRO	The National Archives (Public Record Office), Kew
RO	Record Office

1. The Tremaynes of Collacombe

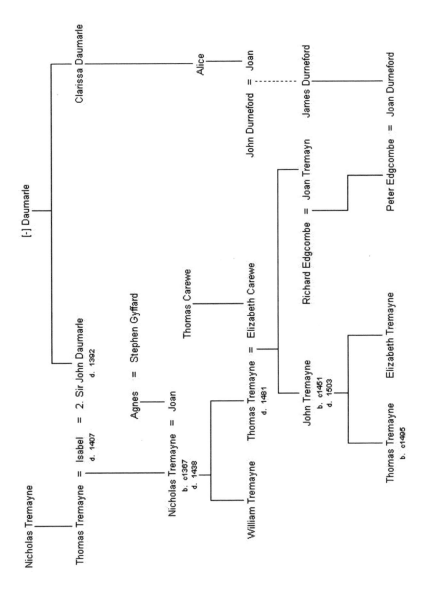

2. The Radfords

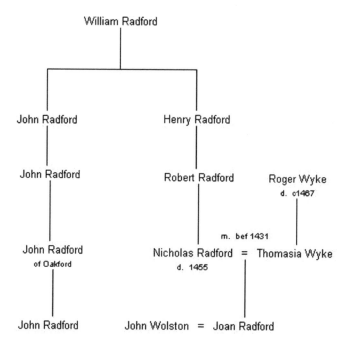

3. Exeter 17th century map

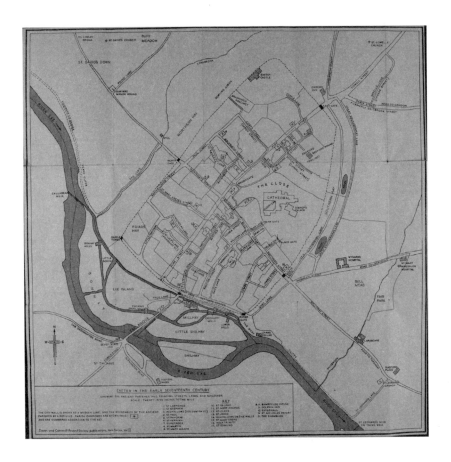

INTRODUCTION

The records edited in this volume illustrate the life of a city
on several days in the first half of the fifteenth century.
More properly, they document the daily life of a number of
inhabitants of a city of varying status and occupations. Much of
the text is concerned with events that were in their nature trivial,
and would rarely be recorded even in private correspondence,
let alone in official documentation. Their survival is thus the
coincidence of two accidents: not only that the record should
have survived mostly intact, but also that events of the kind that
it chronicles should have been deemed of sufficient consequence
to a more weighty matter to be preserved in writing in the first
place.

Behind the recording of this story (or rather, this collection
of stories) lay a dispute. It was one of the disputes over a title
to land that were common in the later middle ages. Men of all
ages and ranks were prone to contest each other's inheritances,
conveyances and seisins, so long as they could afford the cost of
doing so. Yet, by a further coincidence one of the protagonists
of the story was no obscure country gentleman: he was one of
the leading lawyers of his day, and one whose name would some
years after the events detailed here be drawn into political events
on a wider scale.

In the course of the litigation that arose from the dispute in
question, the parties to the quarrel produced witnesses whose
testimony in court can have done little to elucidate the issue in
hand, but whose explanations of how they came to have knowledge
of circumstances supposedly relevant to that issue combine to

produce a unique picture of aspects of the daily lives of individual
15th-century Englishmen from a range of social and professional
backgrounds.

THE TREMAYNE DISPUTE

The disputes and relationships that connected and divided the
parties involved in the inquiry of 1439 were complex. At the
root of the matter ostensibly lay a quarrel between two brothers,
Thomas and William Tremayne, over the manor of North Huish.
In the late 14th century the manor had formed part of the estates
of Sir John Daumarle, one of the leading retainers of Edward
Courtenay, earl of Devon.[1] Daumarle, who was childless, had
settled his estates on feoffees, with instructions that after his
death his lands should fall to his wife, Isabella, during her life,
and then pass to his right heirs. Daumarle's heir general was his
great-niece Joan, the wife of John Durneford, a landowner from
the Plymouth area. In subsequent years Daumarle's feoffees died
one by one, and after Isabella Daumarle's death in 1407 the sole
surviving feoffee, Sir John Daumarle's stepson Nicholas Tremayne,
the fruit of Isabella's first marriage, took the estates for himself.
Attempts by Durneford and his wife to recover their inheritance
in the lawcourts apparently came to nothing, and in November
1417 Durneford formally renounced his claim to North Huish
to Tremayne.[2] Nicholas Tremayne remained in possession of the
manor for more than twenty years, until in March 1438, then over
seventy years old, he settled the manor on his eldest son and heir,
Thomas, in return for an annual rent of £20. He was, however,
barely able to collect the first two terms' installments before his
death in September of the same year.[3]

Now, however, Thomas Tremayne's younger brother, William,
appeared on the scene, and claimed that in a separate transaction
his father had settled North Huish on him. In this, he was
evidently supported by his father's former steward, John Bydelake,
and apparently also by another, more important, player, Roger
Champernon of Bere Ferrers, an influential local esquire and

---

1.   PRO, C1/68/69; C1/7/73; BL, Add. Ch. 64320.
2.   *CIPM*, xix. 452; Devon RO, Tremayne of Collacombe mss, 158M/T508.
3.   Devon RO, Tremayne of Collacombe mss, 158M/E9, T6, T508-10.

former sheriff of Devon. Champernon himself seems to have had designs on the manor of North Huish, and – so talk among his household servants ran – intended to use the feeble William Tremayne to get his way. Through Champernon's good offices William Tremayne's case was taken up by Nicholas Radford, one of the most prominent Devon lawyers of his day. Radford, so one version of events ran, was instrumental in arranging for a copy of Nicholas Tremayne's seal with which a forged deed supporting William Tremayne's title could be sealed.[4]

At this point the sequence of events becomes confused. It seems that the North Huish transaction and Radford's involvement in it had become a talking point among the citizens of Exeter. Certainly, William Tremayne's sudden association with the prominent lawyer had attracted some attention. In addition, the foolish Tremayne and others were openly talking about the forged signet. Radford's clerk, Roger Castell, so the story went, had taken it for repair to the ageing Exeter goldsmith Tilman Cok, who, since his eye-sight was too poor to do the detailed work that was required, had referred them to his associate, Thomas Thorpe. By the late autumn of 1438 Champernon, perhaps with the advice of Radford, had decided to cut his losses. On 15 December 1438 the two men began proceedings for conspiracy and trespass in the mayor's court of Exeter not only against Thomas Tremayne, but also against William Tremayne and John Bydelake, all of whom were arrested and imprisoned.[5] Radford in particular had good reason to be annoyed at the slur on his character that the charge of forging Nicholas Tremayne's signet represented: forgery of seals had long been an offence, and under a statute of 1413 the manufacture and publication of false deeds was also punishable by two years of imprisonment.[6]

The experience of spending an uncomfortable Christmas under lock and key may have had a salutary effect on William Tremayne

---

4. PRO, C1/39/142; C254/143/87; CP40/714, rot. 320.
5. Devon RO, Exeter mayor's court roll 17-18 Hen. VI, rot. 11. It was probably at this stage in proceedings before the mayor's court that torches were provided to light the guildhall: Exeter receiver's account 17-18 Hen. VI.
6. *Statutes of the Realm* (11 vols., London, 1810–28), ii. 170-71, 202; *RP*, ii. 308; iv. 10, 378.

who now took his brother's side, but at any rate Radford and Champernon were, it appears, no longer interested in him, and on 5 January the charges against him and Bydelake were dropped.[7] Thomas Tremayne, by contrast, had in the interim acquired a powerful supporter in the person of Sir John Speke, a local knight who in his youth had studied the law at Lincoln's Inn. Through his paternal grandmother, Speke was a distant relative of John Bydelake's wife, but he seems to have harboured a grudge against Nicholas Radford which may have played a part in drawing him to the Tremaynes' side: even in the summer of 1438 the two men were bickering over property at Dulverton, East Dowlish and West Dowlish in Somerset.[8]

In spite of an apparent agreement to submit the matter to the arbitration of Thomas Courtenay, earl of Devon, the focus of the litigation between Thomas Tremayne, Radford and Champernon now shifted to the court of Chancery at Westminster. Here, Tremayne presented a petition which outlined Radford's and Champernon's fraudulent activities and provided details of dates and places when these had taken place.[9] Radford and Champernon for their part responded in similar detail, providing an alibi for the dates put forward by Tremayne. The Chancellor, Bishop John Stafford of Bath and Wells, was no stranger to Exeter and its region, having been a residentiary canon of Exeter for ten years from 1414 until his elevation to the episcopate in 1424, but even he felt unable to decide between the detailed submissions made by the parties. As a consequence, on 12 March 1439 Bishop Edmund Lacy of Exeter, John Cobethorn, dean of Exeter, and Walter Colles, precentor of Exeter cathedral, were commissioned to try and unravel the web of allegations and counter-allegations.[10] Over a period of three months from 1 April to 10 July the commissioners sat at Exeter cathedral and recorded the evidence of a host of witnesses, ranging from the earl of Devon and his household servants to common labourers and servants.

In the event, the evidence collected during this time can have

---

7. Devon RO, Exeter mayor's court roll 17-18 Hen. VI, rots. 12, 15, 15d, 16, 17.
8. PRO, CP40/714, rots. 135, 363; CP40/715, rot. 36.
9. PRO, C1/39/142; C254/143/87.
10. *CPR*, 1436–41, p. 273.

done little to settle the questions before the Chancellor: the witnesses fielded by the parties produced, as might be expected, contradictory versions of events. If Bishop Stafford ever reached a verdict, no record of it has survived. Meanwhile, the parties continued their bickering in the lawcourts. Even while the Exeter commissioners were taking evidence, Nicholas Radford brought an action of maintenance (a suit at law against a non-lawyer supporting a party to another suit) against Sir John Speke in the court of common pleas and demanded £4000 in damages. A jury was summoned to try the matter, and a panel returned by the sheriff, Sir James Chudleigh, but Speke lost little time in complaining to the Chancellor of the partiality of the named jurors.[11] At the same time, separate litigation brought by Thomas Tremayne against Radford, his son-in-law John Wolston, his clerk Roger Castell, the goldsmith Thomas Thorpe, the Exeter scriveners Nicholas Stoddon and William Speare and several associates also continued in the court of common pleas.[12] In the spring of 1440, Radford also turned his attention to some of the other parties involved in the affair: in mid April he appeared in the Exeter mayor's court to charge his erstwhile associate, the goldsmith Thomas Thorpe, with having detained unspecified goods.[13] Litigation between Radford and Speke over a range of issues pending between them was on-going in 1440. As was frequently the case with suits in the 15th-century common-law courts, no verdicts are recorded, and the matter simply petered out, perhaps in part as a result of Speke's death in November 1441.

THE INQUIRY OF 1439

The year 1439 was a busy one in Exeter and its hinterland. The inquiry into the Radford-Tremayne affair was not the only one to be conducted there. In April the earl of Devon, Bishop Lacy, Sir Philip Courtenay, William Wynard, the recorder of Exeter, Nicholas Radford, and the precentor of Exeter cathedral, Walter Colles, had unsuccessfully gathered the gentry and clergy of the

11. PRO, CP40/714, rot. 320; C1/45/236.
12 PRO, CP40/715, rot. 247d.
13. Devon RO, Exeter mayor's court roll 17-18 Hen. VI, rot. 35.

shire to persuade them to make a loan to Henry VI's increasingly
desperate administration.[14] In June commissioners including
Precentor Colles were dispatched to Plymouth to take the muster
of the earl of Huntingdon's army bound for Gascony.[15] Later
that month Sir John Dynham of Nutwell and Richard Holand
of Cowick were ordered to investigate the mismanagement of the
property of the alien priory at Cowick, and the following month
other commissioners were appointed to look into an incursion by
Dynham into Sir William Bonville's property at Woodbury near
his own seat of Nutwell.[16] In October yet other commissioners
headed by the mayor, Benet Drew, examined witnesses as to the
will of Master Roger Bolter, Colles' predecessor as precentor, and
there were also two inquiries into an alleged attack by Sir John
Speke on one John Laurence at Ottery St. Mary.[17]

In view of these distractions, it is not surprising that the
commissioners in the Tremayne-Radford inquiry took more than
three months, from 1 April to 10 July to interview witnesses and
to record their statements. The 86 individuals whose testimony
survives came from every walk of life and all ranks of society. At
the pinnacle of the social hierarchy stood unquestionably the earl
of Devon who appeared in person to give evidence. With him came
his stepfather, John Botreaux, his esquire, Nicholas Tremayll, and
several other members of his household, the earl's steward and
understeward, Thomas Welywrought and William Bisshop, his
butler, pantler and wardrober, Richard Nele, Alan Holme and
John Pye, his barber, John Prewe, the usher of his hall, Walter
Owyntyn, and the yeoman Henry Mabbe.

Exeter's ruling élite was represented among the witnesses by
the serving mayor, Benet Drew, and one of the stewards, Vincent
Hert, two former mayors, John Coteler and John Shillingford,
and three former receivers, John Crosse, Richard Orynge and
William Upton. Several other witnesses either had or would later
serve in the lesser city offices of alderman, bridge warden, gate-

---

14. PRO, SC1/58/48; *CPR*, 1436–41, p. 250; Hannes Kleineke, 'The
     Commission *de Mutuo Faciendo* in the Reign of Henry VI', *EHR*, cxvi
     (2001), 1-30, pp. 1-2.
15. *CPR*, 1436–41, p. 274.
16. *CPR*, 1436–41, p. 314.
17. *CPR*, 1436–41, pp. 274, 370; PRO, C47/7/6(1); C244/25/46.

keeper and serjeant at mace. A range of trades and occupations were represented among the witnesses. They included the notary Drew, the apothecary Upton, the goldsmith Thomas Thorpe, the glasier William Undy, several lawyers, five tailors, two saddlers and a spurrier. A large number of witnesses came from less prestigious occupations. There were seven skinners, five tuckers, five weavers, two cordwainers, two carpenters, two blacksmiths, a brewer, a hostler, a locksmith and a panbeater. At the bottom of the social scale ranked John Wilscomb, a 'carrier of sacks', two labourers, and Richard Roland, servant to the weaver Richard Nahilyn.

The clergy accounted for fourteen witnesses, including the incumbents of the Exeter parishes of St. Mary Major and St. Olave, John Boryngton and James Richard, and those of the parishes of Cruwys Morchard, Lezant, Poughill, Roseash and Whitstone, John Maior, John Wolston, Robert Nywenham, John Hoigge and Piers Wynterborn, as well as a friar, Dr. John Courteys, John Michell, one of the annuellars of Exeter cathedral, and William Cheke, Roger Champernon's household chaplain. Perhaps the most important of the clerical witnesses was the notary Master John Thryng, procurator general of the bishop of Exeter's consistory court and registrar of the archdeaconry of Barnstaple.

In terms of the witnesses' provenance, Exeter naturally provided the greatest number, accounting for more than half of the men examined. Nine witnesses lived in the north-eastern parishes of St. Martin, St. Laurence and St. Stephen; the large north-western parish of St. Paul housed a further four; nine came from the central parishes of All Hallows Goldsmith Street, St. Kerrian, St. Petrock, St. Pancras, and St. George, while seven were drawn from the southern and south-western parishes of St. Mary Steps, St. John, St. Olave, Holy Trinity, and the great parish of St. Mary Major. The extramural parishes of St. David, St. Thomas and St. Sidwell accounted for a further five witnesses. The involvement of the earl of Devon in the disputed events meant that a large number of the witnesses who came from outside the city were members of the comital household or came from towns and villages near Tiverton like Cruwys Morchard, Radford's own home at Poughill or the Palton seat at Uplowman. Another group of witnesses came from western Devon, where Thomas Tremayne and Roger Champernon respectively resided at Collacombe (in Lamerton) and Bere Ferrers, and from neighbouring Tavistock.

The ages attributed to witnesses at inquiries are notoriously unreliable, and external evidence shows this to be true of the ages given in the inquiry of 1439, but they do at least afford an impression of the rough spread of age groups examined. Whereas proofs of age had to rely on men who had been of sufficient age more than twenty years earlier to be able to bear witness to a birth or baptism, the relatively short time that had passed since the events with which the Exeter commissioners of 1439 were concerned meant that a large proportion of the witnesses were comparatively young men. Just four of them were said to be aged 60 and over, and a further twelve 50 and more. By contrast, 25 of the witnesses were thought not to have reached their thirtieth birthday, almost half of them said to be younger than 25. A further 21 men gave their age as 30 and over and another four claimed to be between 33 and 36. Seventeen men were said to be between 40 and 48. This spread of ages meant that the witnesses examined at Exeter were on average just 35 years old.

NICHOLAS RADFORD

Central to the depositions taken at Exeter in the spring of 1439 was the colourful character of Nicholas Radford, one of the leading lawyers of his day. Born in the latter years of Richard II's reign, he had trained in the law, probably at one of the Inns of Court in Holborn near London. He had rapidly made his mark in the profession and by the end of Henry V's reign he cut a familiar figure among the throngs of the men-of-law who practised in the Westminster law courts. In spite of his increasing renown, he did not, however, begin to scale the career ladder of the Westminster judiciary by joining the ranks of the serjeants at law, preferring instead to reap the greater financial rewards available to the apprentices at law who provided counsel to their clients both in the central courts and in the localities. In his native south-west Radford's professional services were much sought after, and his clients included (as well as lesser men) the leaders of local society: the Courtenay earls of Devon and the rising landowner Sir William (later Lord) Bonville. His private practice aside, Radford for many years served the Crown as a justice of the peace and as counsel to the duchy of Lancaster, and from 1442 held office as recorder of the prosperous merchant city of Exeter, the undisputed capital of the west. As some of the witness statements printed below demonstrate, Radford was not above occasional sharp practice, and as much as his employers valued his services, so others came to detest him. Crucially, as relations between Thomas Courtenay, earl of Devon, and William, Lord Bonville (who had taken pride of place in south-western society during the earl's minority), deteriorated from the early 1440s, so Courtenay's relationship with his erstwhile counsellor Radford also turned sour. The outcome was Radford's brutal murder by the earl's men (led by his eldest son, Sir Thomas Courtenay) on the night of 23 October 1455 in a midnightly scene vividly described in a petition presented by Radford's cousin in Parliament within a few weeks of the event.[18] According to this version of events, about midnight on the night in question Radford was awoken by the noise of Sir Thomas's almost 100-strong following, who had set fire to the pale surrounding his house at Upcott. Having ascertained the identity of the rabble's leader, Radford agreed to let Sir Thomas in, offered him food and drink, and spent some time in conversation with him. Unbeknown to him, Courtenay's men in the interim sacked the house, loading the lawyer's portable property on to his horses, and even tipping his invalid wife out of bed in order to take the sheets. Radford only appears to have become aware of what had transpired

---

18. *The Commons 1386–1421*, iv. 168-70; Hannes Kleineke, 'Radford, Nicholas', in *The History of Parliament: The Commons 1422–61* ed. L.S. Clark (forthcoming). For the Bonville-Courtenay dispute, see G.H. Radford, 'The Fight at Clyst in 1455', *Transactions of the Devon Association*, xliv (1912), 252-65; Martin Cherry, 'The Struggle for Power in Mid-Fifteenth Century Devonshire', in *Patronage, the Crown and the Provinces in Later Medieval England* ed. R.A. Griffiths (Gloucester, 1981), 123-44; *idem*, 'The Courtenay Earls of Devon: The Formation and Disintegration of a Late Medieval Aristocratic Affinity', *Southern History*, i (1979), 71-97; *idem*, 'The Crown and Political Community in Devonshire, 1377–1461' (Univ. of Wales, Swansea, Ph.D. thesis, 1981); Hannes Kleineke, '"þe Kynges Cite": Exeter in the Wars of the Roses', in *Conflicts, Consequences and the Crown in the Late Middle Ages: The Fifteenth Century VII* ed. L.S. Clark (Woodbridge, 2007), 137-56.

when Sir Thomas ordered him to accompany him to Tiverton, and a servant reported the theft of the lawyers' horses. Radford remonstrated with Courtenay, who rode off, leaving his men to hack the old man to death.[19]

The witness statements recorded at Exeter in 1439 afford a glimpse of the lawyer's life beyond his professional activities. Several men had memories of Radford's management and improvement of his property at Upcott. In March 1438 the locksmith Walter Lokier had been consulted by Radford regarding the best type of lock for the back door of his mansion, while the following October the carpenter Richard Isaak had been hired by him to set up a porch at the south door of his hall at Upcott. Two other men recalled seeing Radford that same October overseeing the efforts of the tenants cleaning the mill ditch there, carrying a staff in his hand. Others had witnessed something of the lawyer's daily life. Walter Lokier recalled coming to Radford's town house and finding him in his parlour reading a book. Similarly, the labourer Robert Counseill had seen him sitting under a vine in his Exeter garden early on an April morning reading in a scroll. Several others had seen Radford fox hunting at Woolfardisworthy and Poughill in October 1438. About the same time John Hoigge, the parson of Roseash, had seen Radford at Poughill where he had partaken of the church ale. He had evidently enjoyed himself, for when the cordwainer John Dyrwill arrived at Upcott between 6 and 7 on the following morning to fetch Radford and his hounds to join the earl of Devon for a hunting party, he saw the lawyer come down from his chamber in a state of some disarray – ungirt and

---

19. The dramatic story of Nicholas Radford's murder at the hands of the earl of Devon's sons was first told by his kinsman and heir John Radford of Cadleigh within weeks of the killing in a petition to the King. From this petition the account of the crime subsequently found its way on to the record of the court of King's bench. The Latin version found among the ancient indictments of the court was partially edited by G.H. Radford in 1903 (G.H. Radford, 'Nicholas Radford, 1385(?)–1455', *Transactions of the Devonshire Association*, xxxv (1903), 251-78, at pp. 273-78). Detailed modern accounts of the murder are found in Robin Storey's account of the unravelling of Henry VI's kingship, and in more recent biographies of Nicholas Radford in the *History of Parliament* and the *Oxford Dictionary of National Biography*.

with his hose about his knees. The regular stream of messengers arriving at Radford's mansion at all hours to summon him into the earl of Devon's presence provides an instructive context for the circumstances of the lawyer's murder fifteen years later. In the light of the frequent and often whimsical demands made by the earl (such as the early-morning summons to an impromptu hunting party) Radford's ostensibly irrational decision to offer hospitality to the earl's son in the face of the open attack on his property and his agreement to accompany him to see the earl in spite of the evidence of the ransacking of his house becomes more intelligible.

EXETER IN THE FIFTEENTH CENTURY

Compared with some of the great commercial centres of other parts of England, early fifteenth-century Exeter was at best a second rate city: in terms of its population it was only half the size of Salisbury, about a quarter of the size of York or Bristol, and could not remotely hope to compete with the city of London. Yet, in its own region the city was unrivalled as a commercial, administrative and religious centre. Through its port of Topsham it conducted a busy overseas trade which expanded considerably in the second half of the century, it housed a staple with its own mayor and bailiffs and staple court where bonds of statute staple could be recorded, and it provided an important trading centre for the supply of its hinterland. The great cathedral of St. Peter housed the throne of the episcopal see that covered the entire south-western peninsula of England, while no other town in the diocese could boast a similar conglomeration of religious houses and parish churches. Apart from the Benedictine priory of St. Nicholas, the Cluniac house of St. James, the nunnery at Polsloe and the alien priory at Cowick (suppressed by Henry V, and after its refoundation in 1440 variously granted to Eton college and Tavistock abbey by successive monarchs), Franciscans and Dominicans both had friaries within or just outside the city walls, while the citizens could turn to more than twenty parish churches and chapels for their devotions. In addition there were the hospital of St. John the Baptist by the East Gate, the leper house of St. Mary Magdalene outside the South Gate and the charitable foundations of Simon Grendon and later William

Wynard.[20] The Norman castle of Rougemont in the north-eastern corner of the city provided the meeting place for the Devon county court and the headquarters of the sheriffs of Devon, and the city's importance as the centre of royal administration in the county was further emphasized by the regular sessions of assize and of the peace, and the ad-hoc inquiries to which it played host.

Exeter was governed by an official hierarchy headed by a mayor, receiver and two stewards elected annually on Monday after Michaelmas. They were assisted by a host of junior officials and a council of 12 (increased in size to 24 between 1435 and 1438 and again after 1450), elected at the same time. These office holders were drawn from the body of the freemen of the city.[21] There were three routes to the freedom: apprenticeship, patrimony, and redemption (payment of a fine), and the latter route – by far the most common – ensured that the civic élite that ruled Exeter did not become an impermeable oligarchy.[22] If the permeability of Exeter's social hierarchy ensured by and large peaceful relations between the city's different economic groups, the first half of the 15th century saw conflict in another arena: between the city's laity

20. Nicholas Orme, 'Access and Exclusion: Exeter Cathedral, 1300–1540', in *Freedom of Movement in the Middle Ages* ed. Peregrine Horden (Donington, 2007), 267-86, pp. 267-70; J.M. James, 'The Norman Benedictine Alien Priory of St. George, Modbury, AD c. 1135–1480', *Transactions of the Devonshire Association*, cxxxi (1999), 81-104, pp. 93-97; Ethel Lega-Weekes, 'The Pre-Reformation History of the Priory of St. Katherine, Polsloe, Exeter', *Transactions of the Devonshire Association*, lxvi (1934), 181-99.

21. Bertie Wilkinson, *The Mediaeval Council of Exeter* (Manchester, History of Exeter Research Group Monograph no. 4, 1931), pp. xxiv-xxxiii, 1-6; L.C. Attreed, *The King's Towns. Identity and Survival in Late Medieval English Boroughs* (New York et al., 2001), pp. 21-22; *The History of Parliament: The Commons 1386–1421*, ed. J.S. Roskell, Linda Clark and Carole Rawcliffe (4 vols., Stroud, 1992), i. 350.

22. *Exeter Freemen 1266–1967* ed. M.M. Rowe and A.M. Jackson (Exeter, Devon and Cornwall Record Society extra ser. i, 1973), pp. xiii-xvii; Maryanne Kowaleski, 'The commercial Dominance of a medieval provincial Oligarchy: Exeter in the late fourteenth century', *Mediaeval Studies*, xlvi (1984), 355-84, repr. in *The English Medieval Town: A Reader in Urban History 1200–1540* ed. Richard Holt and Gervase Rosser (1990), 184-215, pp. 209-13; *eadem, Local markets and Regional Trade in Medieval Exeter* (Cambridge, 1995), pp. 96-99.

and clergy, or more properly between the lay and ecclesiastical authorities. For much of the period in question the city fathers sought to assert their authority in the bishop's extramural liberty of St. Sidwell's and the cathedral liberty within Exeter itself. At the time of the inquiry of 1439 the citizens had only recently conceded defeat over St. Sidwell's, and a decade later they were forced to do likewise over the cathedral close. The misbehaviour of individual members of the clergy in the city and of citizens within the close was occasionally cited as one of the causes for the dispute, but the reality seems to have been rather more mundane. If the accounts of the civic receiver and the letters of Mayor John Shillingford speak of a civic preoccupation with the quest for jurisdiction within the ecclesiastical liberties, it seems that the lives of most inhabitants of Exeter remained largely untouched by the disagreements of their rulers, an impression borne out by some of the testimony recorded in 1439.[23]

The statements taken afford a fascinating insight into the communal life of Exeter and the surrounding countryside in the late 1430s. Many of the occurrences that the witnesses remembered were routine parts of daily life. The various trades of the witnesses and other citizens loomed large. Richard Sporiour recalled his failure to sell a pair of new spurs to Roger Champernon, but had at the same time succeeded in supplying his goods to two of the esquire's retainers. The brewer Roger Holecombe remembered purchasing spices from the mercer John Kelvelegh on a specified afternoon, and also told of the supply of church bells to Guernsey by the bell-founder Robert Norton.

Both annual and unusual events in the city's calendar provided a time-frame to which the witnesses might relate their testimony. On the first Monday after Michaelmas the mayoral elections had taken place as usual: in accordance with custom, the occasion was announced by the blowing of a horn, as the pan beater William Coppe told the inquiry. In the run-up to the Palm Sunday festivities the parish clerk of St. Stephen's had collected the keys of the parish church from Philip Yerle, presumably then serving as church

23. M.E. Curtis, *Some Disputes between the City and the Cathedral Authorities of Exeter* (Manchester, 1932), *passim*; *Letters and Papers of John Shillingford, Mayor of Exeter, 1447–50* ed. S.A. Moore (London, Camden Soc. o.s. ii, 1871), *passim*.

warden, to prepare the palms. Rather more exceptional was the visit of King Henry VI's uncle, Humphrey, duke of Gloucester, in the spring of 1438, a major occasion which had dominated the concerns of the civic élite. More common, but nevertheless memorable, was one of the periodic bouts of the plague that struck Exeter and its hinterland in 1438. As a maritime region the south-west was particularly susceptible to the spread of epidemic disease by its large transient population, who came and went, bringing infections from other parts of England and the European continent. Interestingly, a number of people from the countryside sought refuge from the plague in the city, where presumably health care provision was thought to be better. Thus, the Poughill tailor William Butte recalled how in April 1438 Nicholas Radford had moved from Upcott into Exeter on account of the plague, and had asked him to stand in for his pantler, who along with his other servants was remaining at the lawyer's country seat, while another tailor from Poughill, Thomas Skynner, remembered coming to the city to visit two children of John Wolston's whom he had previously fostered, but who had also been brought to Exeter on account of the epidemic.

While most of the witnesses were specific as to the days on which particular events had occurred, the accuracy with which they felt able to time events within individual days varied. A number of men made reference to particular hours 'of the clock', while others referred, perhaps more explicitly, to hours 'of the bell'. Certainly, there were in Exeter a number of public time pieces by which individuals might be guided, including some in parish churches like St. Petrock's, the clock of which possessed a chime.[24]

Several witnesses illustrated the interaction of individuals of widely differing social ranks. In response to the courteous greeting offered by the simple cordwainer John Stephyn, both the wealthy esquire Roger Champernon and even his less cultivated companion, William Tremayne, who within moments is seen rudely pushing past the skinner John Pyke, causing him to drop his leeks, turn back to return Stephyn's greeting. Charity (or at least neighbourliness) on a greater scale is exemplified by the

---

24. Devon RO, Exeter, St. Petrock's Parish, churchwardens' accounts 2946A-99PW1, m. 4; 2946A-99PW2, mm. 44, 46

weaver Henry Hornysbowe, who is caring for the sick and ageing parson of St. Kerrian, Thomas Cook. Hospitality is apparently freely and widely offered. When the former mayor John Coteler asks Radford about his recent move of house, he is immediately invited to visit and partake of a drink, and when he does so on the same day, they are joined by the priest Sir John Wolston. Even in Radford's absence at the Cornish assizes in April 1438, Robert Wilford is daily entertained to drinks by the lawyer's wife at their new town house in Northgate Street. On their arrival in Exeter from the comital residence at Colcombe, William Bisshop and Roger Champernon are offered refreshment in the house of Richard Orynge.

DEVONSHIRE IN THE 1430s

Several of the witnesses who attested Radford's absence from Exeter on the dates in question afford glimpses of wider county society towards the end of Henry VI's minority. The death of Hugh Courtenay, earl of Devon, in June 1422 had left his son and heir, Thomas, a minor. Much of the political authority of the Crown which might otherwise have been vested in an adult earl came to be vested in a group of landowners headed by Sir Walter (from 1426 Lord) Hungerford, which also included the Devon knights Sir William Bonville and the earl's cousin, Sir Philip Courtenay of Powderham. The prestige of the Courtenay family in local society was maintained by the earl's uncle, Sir Hugh Courtenay of Haccombe, until his death in 1425, thereafter the focus shifted to some degree back to 'my old lady of Devonshire', the dowager countess Anne who held a substantial share of the estates of the earldom in jointure and shared the comital seat of Tiverton with her second husband, John Botreaux. The young earl was granted livery of his lands in 1433, still aged only 18, but with the comital castle of Tiverton still in his mother's hands, was forced to establish himself at the lesser seat of Colcombe (in Coliton).[25] The Exeter witness statements paint a picture of the earl's establishment. It was made up of a few older experienced officers, such as the steward of the lands, John Coppleston, who

---

25. *CP*, iv. 326-27; Cherry, 'The Courtenay Earls of Devon,' pp. 95-96.

had held the same post by royal appointment during Thomas Courtenay's minority, but also included many younger servants, who were perhaps better matched to their master in temperament, and who could be expected to remain in his service throughout their lives.

It is generally accepted that the roots of the violence which engulfed Devonshire in the 1450s lay in Earl Thomas's loss of status in local society during his long minority, and his need to reassert himself after coming of age. Against this background, it is interesting to see the very ordinariness of county life depicted by the witnesses of 1439. Individual men served both the earl and his mother and stepfather. They also maintained close connexions with a variety of leading landowners, some of them part of the family circle of the earl's cousin, Sir Philip Courtenay of Powderham, like Roger Champernon of Bere Ferrers, Sir James Chudleigh, and Sir William Palton, but also others, like Sir John Dynham of Nutwell, after the earl the wealthiest landowner in Devon. Sir Philip Courtenay is seen dispatching his half-brother, William Chuddelegh, to invite his aunt, Lady Palton, to attend the churching of his wife. Having attended this event, the lady continues on a pilgrimage to Crediton and on the way home accepted the hospitality of both the earl's steward, the lawyer John Coppleston, and Nicholas Radford. The men paying their respects to the young earl include Roger Champernon, and a variety of lesser men, but also the Hampshire knight Sir Stephen Popham. More mundane events are also in evidence. The earl's steward William Bisshop comes to Colyton to hold the manor court, and John Wolston does the same at Bradninch and Poughill, and takes the opportunity to sample the church ale. The collegiate church at Crediton features as a local centre of religious activity. Lady Palton's pilgrimage apart, the learned Friar John Courteys also recalls a special journey there undertaken in order to preach a sermon.

THE PROBLEM OF VERACITY

The colourful stories told by the witnesses examined at Exeter in 1439 make it tempting to accept the detail they provide as an accurate account of true events, but some caution is necessary.

The difficulties inherent in the interpretation of legal records which in their majority provide partial, biased and often fictitious accounts of events have long been recognised.[26] The peculiar problems presented by collections of depositions similar to that printed below have been stressed by historians, not least with reference to the evidence purportedly given by individual witnesses in the proofs of age of feudal tenants in chief. Many of the stories recorded, it has been demonstrated, were generic, and did not reflect true events recalled from more than two decades before. In some instances, royal officials might even simply copy older documents almost verbatim.[27] While the events related by the witnesses at Exeter in 1439 were more recent than those recorded in proofs of age, and the length and detail of what was deposed makes it unlikely that it was a simple copy of another collection of evidence, the testimony given presents a different problem. Attempts to pervert the course of justice were endemic in late medieval litigation. The law was treated by many as an elaborate game in which the party who could most skilfully stack the cards in its favour would prevail. Bribes to undersheriffs and bailiffs produced packed juries,[28] and even independent jurors could be persuaded by monetary rewards to read out verdicts

26. On the common law records, see e.g. *Legal Records and the Historian*, ed. J.H. Baker (London, 1978), p. 3; P.C. Maddern, *Violence and Social Order: East Anglia 1422–1442* (Oxford, 1992), pp. 27-31, 237; Christine Carpenter, *Locality and Polity* (Cambridge, 1992), pp. 705-09.

27. R.C. Fowler, 'Legal Proofs of Age', *EHR*, xxii (1907), 101-3; M.T. Martin, 'Legal Proofs of Age', *EHR*, xxii (1907), 526-27; A.E. Stamp, 'Legal Proofs of Age', *EHR*, xxix (1914), 323-24; and more recently Simon Payling's reviews of vols. XXII and XXIII of the *Calendar of Inquisitions post Mortem*, *EHR*, cxx (2005), 447-48 and cxxi (2006), 914-15, and Matthew Holford, '"Testimony (to some extent fictitious)": proofs of age in the first half of the fifteenth century', *Historical Research*, lxxxii (2009), 635-54.

28. At the south-western assize sessions held in the five years between September 1424 and August 1429 some 34 juries were dismissed on the grounds of having been packed by a sheriff or under-sheriff: PRO, JUST1/1540, rots. 3, 19d, 28d, 29, 36d, 38d, 39, 40, 41, 43, 44d, 45d, 46, 47d, 52d, 55d, 62, 64d, 70, 71d, 74d, 76d, 78, 78d, 79d, 80, 81d, 83d, 87, 88d, 90d, 92d, 94, 95. For earlier examples, see JUST1/1519, rots. 15d, 53d, 77d, 94d.

readily provided in writing.[29] Within months of the Exeter
inquiry of 1439 the corruption of sheriffs and undersheriffs in
the empannelling of partial juries became the subject of a petiton
of the parliamentary Commons to the Crown.[30]

The witnesses who appeared at Exeter in 1439 were no exception, as the statements made by some of their number plainly
demonstrate. As might be expected, the two groups of men
respectively produced by the parties produced conflicting stories
as to Nicholas Radford's whereabouts in Lent of 1438, and several
witnesses even gave an indication why this should have been so:
William Tremayne had made an elaborate effort to buy favourable
testimony. Thus, the skinner John Person described how Tremayne
had approached him in Exeter cathedral and offered him 40*d.* if he
would depose that he had seen Radford in Exeter on Thursday and
Friday before Palm Sunday 1438, and had grown angry when he
had refused. Another skinner, John Husset, had been approached
by a group of men of Tremayne's party who had offered him the
large sum of 20*s.* if he agreed to testify that Radford had been in
the house of the tailor Richard Orynge on the Friday in question,
and some of them had even promised him as much as 100*s.*
Some of the bribes were more carefully masked. The blacksmith
Richard Ree recounted how the tailor John Watte had offered to
pay him 2*s.* for a 'palotte' which he had previously bought from
him and paid for in full, as well as 14*d.* for earnings lost if he

---

29. E.g. PRO, CP40/756, rot. 370; KB27/836, rot. 72. Rare evidence of
     contemporary attitudes towards such sharp practices is provided by a
     law suit brought in the court of common pleas in the summer of 1456.
     In the course of an action between one John Barnburgh and the Surrey
     esquire Thomas Gower, so it was claimed, both Gower and his opponent's
     attorney, Robert Forster, had approached some of the empaneled jurors
     and provided them with various points of evidence in support of their
     respective cases. Forster for his part stated that he had overheard
     Gower declare deliberate falsehoods, and had reproached him for this
     conduct, saying to him that to misinform the jurors in this way this was
     dishonourable and shameful, and that he ought to consider his honour.
     Gower erupted, told Forster that his honour was none of his concern, and
     threatened him with violence unless he would shut up. The justices agreed
     with Forster's version of events, and committed Gower to the Fleet prison.
     PRO, CP40/782, rot. 323.
30. *Rotuli Parliamentorum* ed. J. Strachey (6 vols., London, 1783), v. 29.

would testify to Radford's presence in Exeter on Tuesday after Michaelmas 1438, and how he had claimed to have 'bought' a pair of spurs from Richard Sporiour on similar terms. Likewise, Ree had heard from his putative kinsman John Ree that he had been paid 40d. to appear as a witness for Tremayne. Principal among Tremayne's recruiting sergeants had been one Philip Yerle. The tucker John Bate described how Yerle had offered him a week's wages if he would testify to seeing Radford in Exeter on Monday after Michaelmas, while the skinner Nicholas Trenewith had been approached by William Tremayne and Philip Yerle one day during Lent 1439 and told him that if he would come to the cathedral on the following morning and corroborate the evidence given by others he and a hundred more should have 2d. for their pains. Concerned about perjuring himself, Trenewith had refused, and had heard no more of the matter until the following Sunday, when he had met Yerle in St. Stephen's church, who had told him that he had disbursed no less than £10 to various witnesses.

The most elaborate account was that of the young tucker William Batyn, who was serving as a journeyman to Richard Wode. On Monday in Holy Week of 1439 Wode had told him and his fellows that he had no work for them the following day, but that he would nevertheless pay them a shilling each, if they would agree to go to the cathedral and give the testimony that Sir John Speke and William Tremayne would ask them to give. Batyn, like Trenewith, had been concerned about perjuring himself, but Wode had reassured him that there would be a hundred witnesses for their part (including Batyn's own father and other men known to him) of whom only four or five would be sworn. On the following morning Batyn had encountered William Tremayne near the East Gate of Exeter, and had been promised a noble if he would procure a further four witnesses. Both Tremayne and his agent Yerle had been busy: they had disbursed all the ready cash available to them. Later on, Batyn had been among the witnesses whom Tremayne assembled at the principal statue of St. Peter in the cathedral for a final briefing. Those who lived in the North Gate quarter were told to say that they had seen Radford in Exeter on the Monday in question, those living in the High Street towards the East Gate on the Tuesday, and those dwelling outside the East Gate on Wednesday. Yet, Radford had not let the grass grow under his feet either. On the following Wednesday (in Holy Week 1439)

Tremayne had come to the stall of Batyn's father in the parish of
St. Pancras and had summoned all his supporters to the cathedral,
for – as he said – Radford had come with more than forty bondmen
prepared to give evidence in his favour.

All of the witnesses examined were nevertheless at pains to
emphasize their credibility. Each closed his statement by declaring
that he had not been corrupted, and several went even further. The
witnesses who elaborated on the bribes they had been offered aside,
several stressed that they had only been promised compensation
for the earnings lost by their attendance at the inquiry. Several
men expressed concern about being asked to perjure themselves;
a number sought to corroborate their evidence by employing
particular formulae. Thus, Friar John Courteys, so the court
recorded, made his statement '*in verbo sacerdocij*'. Some nineteen
witnesses (Richard Orynge, Benedict Drew, John Shillingford,
John Ree, Henry Hornysbowe, Philip Yerle, Richard Roland,
John Brasutor, Richard Wode, Robert Wilford, John Person, John
Bisshop, Thomas Thorpe, John Colmestorre, William Upton, and
the priests William Cheke, John Boryngton, and James Richard
all gave evidence 'in vertu of [their] sacrament'. The parson of
Poughill, Robert Nywenham, specified 'his sacrament made with
his right honde uppon the crosse and *Te igitur*'.

If the witness statements recorded at Exeter in 1439 cannot
without exception be regarded as strictly factual accounts of real
events, they are nevertheless not without value. Crucially, they
were statements that appeared credible to the royal commissioners
before whom they were taken, all of them educated men with
years of experience of Exeter city life. We may thus assume
that the occurrences that the witnesses described struck them
as representative of life in their city and county: if they do not
represent (in von Ranke's terms) events 'as they properly were',
they do at least illustrate daily life as it might properly have been.

THE TEXTS

The principal document edited in the following forms part of the
normal process of the Westminster court of Chancery. Proceedings
in Chancery were normally begun by a petition to the Chancellor
of England. In the early decades of the 15th century such petitions
were still routinely presented in French, but by the 1430s English

had already established itself as the language used by the parties in the court.[31] In response to such a petition, the court would normally issue a writ of *sub poena*, instructing the defendant to appear in court on a set day to answer the charges against him, or of *corpus cum causa*, instructing a local official to produce an arrested defendant and to state the cause of his arrest. The parties would then be invited to present witnesses and other evidence. On certain occasions, for instance, if one of the parties was deemed to be too old or infirm to make the journey to Westminster, commissioners could be appointed by writ of *dedimus potestatem* to travel to the locality where the dispute in hand had arisen and to take the depositions of defendants or witnesses locally. These commissioners were often issued with detailed interrogatories, lists of articles and questions to put to the witnesses they examined. In the case of the inquiry of 1439, another circumstance intervened to prompt a local inquiry: both parties had supplied extensive and detailed arguments, and it was impossible for the Chancellor, so the King's letters patent appointing commisioners stated, to know the truth. As a result, on a series of days between 1 April and 10 July 1439 Edmund Lacy, bishop of Exeter, John Cobethorn, dean of Exeter cathedral, and Walter Colles, treasurer of the same, sat in the chapter house, the lady chapel and the consistory of the cathedral and heard the sworn evidence of the witnesses brought forward by Thomas Tremayne, Nicholas Radford and Roger Champernon. The commissioners had evidently been supplied with a list of articles to inquire into. This schedule is not known to survive, but is referred to regularly in the record of the witness statements. Equally, the 'bills' submitted by the parties are now lost, but some of their content may be inferred from the testimony of individual witnesses. Thomas Tremayne's bill stipulated that on Thursday before Palm Sunday 1438 Roger Champernon, William

31. Writs (of *sub poena*, *dedimus potestatem* etc.) were issued from Chancery, as from other courts and branches of the king's administration, in Latin. On the language of the Chancery see J.H. Fisher, 'Chancery and the Emergence of Standard Written English in the Fifteenth Century', *Speculum*, lii (1977), 870-99; Malcolm Richardson, 'Henry V, the English Chancery, and Chancery English', *Speculum*, lv (1980), 726-50, and more recently also T.S. Haskett, 'Country Lawyers? The Composers of English Chancery Bills', in *The Life of the Law* ed. Peter Birks (London, 1993), 9-23.

Tremayne, John Colmestorre, John Fitz and others had dined with Radford in his house in Corre Street. It went on to give details of the purported forgery of the title deed to North Huish. It described how William Tremayne had come to Tilman Goldesmyth at Exeter and had asked him to amend a signet displaying an escallop, but had been told to seek the assistance of the younger Thomas Thorpe. Thorpe, so the bill continued, had been informed by Radford's clerk that he and his fellows intended to use the signet to seal a letter, and had agreed to repair it. It mentioned the forgery, and gave details of how on Friday before Michaelmas 1438 William Tremayne had been at Bere Ferrers, where he and Champernon had arranged to send details of the deed's date and it purported witnesses to Exeter in writing. Finally, it also described a scene at John Shillingford's house at Exeter where Radford, William Tremayne and others had been present, and Radford had sought to bribe Tremayne with the sum of 100 nobles. The contents of Radford's submission cannot be established in as much detail, but it appears that he was above all concerned to establish his alibi and prove that he had not been in Exeter on the days in question.

Four related documents have been printed in an appendix to the main text. The first of these is a further petition submitted in Chancery by Thomas Tremayne. By this bill, Tremayne initiated process against Roger Champernon for his part in the purported forgery of the title deeds for North Huish. No records of any further process following this petition is known. The second document is a record of a suit at common law brought in the court of common pleas by Nicholas Radford against Sir John Speke, accusing the latter of breaking the statute of maintenance by lending his support to Thomas and William Tremayne and John Bydelake in the suit that they had brought against Radford in the mayor's court of Exeter. Both Radford and Speke appeared in court at Westminster in person and pleaded their cases, before the sheriff of Devon was ordered to empanel a jury to decide the issue. The third document picks up where this record from the common bench leaves off. It is a further petition in Chancery, by which Sir John Speke complained that Radford had colluded with the sheriff of Devon, James Chudleigh, and his officer, John Kyrton, to have a biased jury returned to Westminster to decide the case between Radford and Speke.

By contrast with the other three, the final document in this collection is only indirectly connected with the inquiry of 1439, to which it relates chiefly in terms of the parties concerned. It is a petition by Thomas Tremayne to the house of lords in either the parliament of 1439–40 or that of 1442.[32] On this occasion, Tremayne sought redress against a far more powerful opponent, Thomas Courtenay, earl of Devon, who – perhaps alerted to the Tremayne inheritance by the dispute of 1439 – had in early November of that year taken possession of the Tremayne manor of Rake by force, while Thomas Tremayne may still have been occupied by the defence of North Huish. It is not known whether the matter was ever debated by the lords. The original petition bears no engrossment to indicate the lords' decision or the royal assent, and was not enrolled on the parliament roll.[33]

THE MANUSCRIPTS

The principal manuscript edited below, The National Archives (Public Record Office), Chancery, Depositions and Answers, C4/39/31, consists of three separate rolls, held together by sewing on the modern guards. Each roll consists of several parchment membranes, sewn together end to end 'Chancery style'. The first roll, approximately 2.30 m (7'6") long and containing the statements of the witnesses appearing for Thomas Tremayne, consists of five membranes, respectively measuring 29.0 x 24.7 cm, 29.2 x 49.5 cm, 29.3 x 50.0 cm, 29.3 x 52.3 cm and 29.6 x 55.2 cm. The shorter second roll, approximately 58 cm (23") long and

---

32. The best concise recent account of parliamentary procedure at the end of the 15th century is P.R. Cavill, *The English Parliaments of Henry VII, 1485–1504* (Oxford, 2009), pp. 146-53. While much of what is set out here applied when Tremayne presented his petition, bill procedure was evolving throughout the 15th century: for petitioning in the earlier period, see A.R. Myers, 'Parliamentary Petitions in the Fifteenth Century', *EHR*, lii (1937), 385-404, 590-613, repr. in *idem, Crown, Household and Parliament in Fifteenth-Century England* ed. C.H. Clough (London, 1985), 1-44, at pp. 13-17; *idem*, 'Some Observations on the Procedure of the Commons in Dealing with Bills in the Lancastrian Period', *University of Toronto Law Journal*, iii (1939), 51-73, repr. in *idem, Crown, Household and Parliament*, ed. Clough, pp. 45-67, and more recently, G. Dodd, *Justice and Grace* (Oxford, 2007).
33. Private acts of perliament were not invariably enrolled on the parliament roll, but nor were unsuccessful bills.

containing the witnesses appearing for Nicholas Radford, is made up of just two membranes, respectively measuring 29.5 x 23.4 cm and 29.3 x 34.5 cm. The third roll, approximately 3.45 m (11'4") long, is incomplete. Whereas the first two rolls have formal headings and notarial attestations at the foot, these are missing on roll 3, the head and foot of which in addition show stitching holes, suggesting that further membranes have been lost. At the foot the text ends with little room to spare, at the had there is a blank space of approximately 10 cm which may have been intended for a heading. The surviving six membranes respectively measure 29.5 x 57.4 cm, 29.3 x 57.0 cm, 29.5 x 58.2 cm, 29.2 x 61.1 cm, 29.1 x 62.3 cm and 29.2 x 52 cm. Only one side of the parchment has been used, the dorses are blank, except for roll 2, which has been endorsed 'Peticiones et examinaciones in cancellaria ao 36° H 6 xxxvj° - H 6' in an early modern hand.

The King's original commission ordering the inquiry has been printed from its enrolment on the Patent Roll (TNA (PRO), Chancery, Patent Rolls, C66/443, m. 14d). Supplementary litigation has been collected from the plea rolls of the court of common pleas, the Early Proceedings of Chancery, and the Ancient Petitions (TNA (PRO), classes C1, CP40 and SC8). These documents correspond to the format normal for their type in the period.

EDITORIAL CONVENTIONS

In the case of the English texts, the inconsistency of the spellings of the originals even within individual depositions evidently recorded by a single scribe makes it impossible to be sure of the intended reading in every instance. This is particularly true of the treatment of the plural and genitive of nouns, variously rendered -*es*, -*is* or -*ys*, and of the abbreviation for *per-* or *par-*. Equally problematic is the interpretation of the various strokes and flourishes with which the scribes routinely adorn individual letters. In many instances, they are quite clearly meaningless, such as, for instance, in the case of the stroke with which the letter 'h' is routinely crossed, even when the abbreviation for '*hab-*' is not intended or required. Similarly, it is impossible to be sure whether the flourishes employed by the scribes to finish of final letters of words are universally decorative or are in some instances intended to represent a final voiceless

-*e*. For the purposes of this edition, editorial intervention has been kept to a minimum, and the flourishes have been treated as such, unless the text clearly requires an expanded ending on grammatical grounds. Common abbreviations have been expanded throughout, and such expansions have been indicated by Italic type. Otherwise, the text preserves the spelling of the original, except that capitalization has been modernised, and a degree of punctuation introduced in lieu of the pointing of the manuscript. The lower-case letters u/v and i/j which are used interchangeably by the scribes have been rendered as in the original. In the case of the Latin texts a linguistic standard can be established, and for this reason the use of u and v has been standardised in the text from the plea roll of the court of common pleas printed in the appendix, and common abbreviations have been silently expanded. As with the English texts, capitalization has been standardised and a degree of punctuation introduced. Throughout this edition, interlinear additions have been indicated by angled brackets (< >), editorial additions other than the expansion of abbreviations (e.g. the supply of text lost by damage to the manuscripts) by square brackets ([ ]).

APPENDIX: BIOGRAPHICAL DETAILS OF WITNESSES AND OTHER INDIVIDUALS MENTIONED IN THE TEXT

Personal names have been given in the form in which they appear in the text. Individuals who have their own entries in this appendix are indicated by an asterisk (*).

AT WILLE, William (*d.*c.1463), of Exeter

An Exeter merchant, At Wille served on the council from 1454–57 and 1461–63 and held office as steward in 1437–38 and 1449–50, as well as representing the city in parliament in 1455 and 1460. Between 1431 and 1447 he also held crown office as searcher first (briefly) in the Cornish district, and subsequently for almost fifteen years at Exeter and Dartmouth. He owned property both in Exeter and in the sea port of Topsham and at his death left at least two sons by his wife Margaret.[1]

1. J.C. Wedgwood and A.D. Holt, *History of Parliament: Biographies of the Members of the Commons House, 1439–1509* (London, 1936), p. 28; H. Kleineke, 'Attwyll, William', in *The History of Parliament: The Commons 1422–61* ed. L.S. Clark (forthcoming); Devon RO, Exeter mayor's court rolls 16-17, 28-29, 33-36 Hen. VI, 1-3 Edw. IV; PRO, CP40/765, rot. 407; CP40/821, rot. 127d; CP40/845, rot. 387; C1/255/36; E122/184/6; E122/185/40; 222, pt. ii, 38/1-2; *Exeter Freemen 1266–1967* ed. M.M. Rowe and A.M. Jackson (Exeter, Devon and Cornwall Record Soc. extra ser. i, 1973), p. 55; *CFR*, xvi. 55, 172; xviii. 61.

BATE, John (*b*.c.1389), of Exeter

Bate was one of several tuckers from the extramural parish of St. David among the witnesses examined in 1439.

BATYN, John (*b*.c.1409), of Exeter

The identification of the tucker John Batyn who resided in the Exeter parish of St. Pancras presents some difficulties, as there were several men of this name active in the city about this time, including a saddler who served as mayor of Exeter in 1423–24 and died in early 1426, and a butcher. It may have been either the tucker or the butcher who served as alderman of the western city quarter in 1445–46 and porter of the west gate in 1446–47 and 1450–51. The age of thirty that Batyn gave at the time of the inquiry of 1439 may have been something of a conservative estimate, as William Batyn*, then believed to be twenty years old, was his son.[2]

BATYN, William (*b*.c.1419), of Exeter

The son of the tucker John Batyn*, William Batyn practised his trade in the parish of St. David outside the North Gate of Exeter.

BENET, John, of Exeter

Like the cordwainer John Stephyn*, Benet lived in the northern quarter of Exeter, where he was periodically presented for breaches of the regulations governing the sale of oats and ale. His daughter had married William Tremayne*.[3]

BISSHOP, John (*b*.c.1393)

Bisshop was a blacksmith attached to the household of William, 3rd Lord Botreaux*, but is not otherwise heard of.

---

2. Devon RO, Exeter mayor's court rolls, 2-3, 4-5, 24-30 Hen. VI; *Exeter Freemen* ed. Rowe and Jackson, pp. 44, 46.
3. Devon RO, mayor's tourn roll 15 Hen. VI, rot. 2.

BISSHOP, William (*b*.c.1399), of Tiverton, Devon

Son of Gilbert Bisshop of Bondleigh, Bisshop trained in the law and by 1423 found employment in the sheriff of Devon's office at Exeter castle. Now residing in the city parish of St. George, he was admitted to the freedom of the city that September and within a few weeks elected one of the city's stewards. He held the same office again three years later in 1426–27 and in the interim served on the city council, but subsequently disappears from the ranks of the citizenry, probably to take up a position in the household of the young earl of Devon, whom he was serving as his understeward at the time of the inquiry of 1439. The second half of Bisshop's career is more difficult to reconstruct. Probably through the earl of Devon's patronage he respectively represented Launceston and Bodmin in the parliaments of 1447 and 1449–50, but even at the time of the latter assembly a man of this name, perhaps the same individual, although it is impossible to be certain, was once again serving as one of the stewards of Exeter. This latter man held the receivership in 1450–51, served on the council of twenty-four from 1452 to 1459 and acted as one of the wardens of the Exe Bridge from 1456 to 1458. He was still alive in the autumn of 1461, when he is last recorded as a participant in the mayoral elections and may have died not long after.[4]

BITHELAKE (Bydelake), John, of Bridestow, Devon

One of the characters central to the events recorded at Exeter in 1439, Bithelake had served as steward of Nicholas Tremayne*, who by his will had left him a silver cup. Along with the two younger Tremaynes he was sued by Nicholas Radford and Roger Champernon in the Exeter mayor's court in December 1438, and was probably instrumental in recruiting Sir John Speke to their side, as his wife, Alice, was the knight's distant kinswoman. His purported involvement in the forgery of Nicholas Tremayne's seal was not the only such accusation he faced: within a year of the inquiry of 1439 the wealthy esquire Thomas Carminowe of Ashwater also charged him with the forgery of muniments.[5]

4. Devon RO, Exeter mayor's court rolls 2 Hen. VI-2 Edw. IV; H. Kleineke, 'Bishop, William', in *The Commons 1422–61* ed. Clark (forthcoming).
5. PRO, CP40/714, rot. 320; CP40/716, rot. 125d; Devon RO, Tremayne of Collacombe MSS, 158M/T6.

BORYNGTON, Sir John (c.1409–1449), of Exeter

Instituted as rector of the Exeter parish church of St. Mary Major at the end of April 1437, Boryngton rapidly passed through the orders of acolyte, subdeacon and deacon in the course of the subsequent year. In March 1438 he had licence to absent himself from his parish for a period of two years for the purpose of studying at Oxford. He was ordained to the priesthood in February 1439, and remained at St. Mary Major until his premature death in 1449, when he was succeeded as rector by Simon Chuddelegh*.[6]

BOTREAUX, John (b.c.1391), of Tiverton, Devon

Probably a younger brother of William, 3rd Lord Botreaux*, John Botreaux made his fortune in 1433 when he married the dowager countess of Devon, Anne Talbot*, and thus gained control of her valuable dower lands, while becoming stepfather to the young earl, Thomas Courtenay*.[7]

BOTREAUX, William (1389–1462), 3rd Lord Botreaux

A peer with landholding through the south-west, the 3rd Lord Botreaux succeeded his father, the 2nd baron, in 1395 aged just six. He fought in Henry V's French wars, and was present at Agincourt. He married twice, firstly Elizabeth, daughter of John, Lord Beaumont, and secondly Margaret, daughter of Thomas, Lord Roos, but had no surviving sons, and at his death his title passed through his daughter Margaret to the Lords Hungerford.[8]

BOWEDON, John, of Exeter

One of the city of Exeter's four serjeants-at-mace from 1437 to 1439, and again from 1454 to 1456, Bowedon may have been the

6. *The Register of Edmund Lacy* ed. F.C. Hingeston-Randolph (2 vols., London, 109-15), i. 220, 339; *The Register of Edmund Lacy, Bishop of Exeter, 1420–1455* ed. G.R. Dunstan (5 vols., Torquay, 1963–72), ii. 42, 79; iv. 166, 171; A.B. Emden, *A Biographical Register of the University of Oxford* (3 vols., Oxford, 1957–59), i. 223.
7. *CP*, iv. 326. Botreaux must be distinguished from his uncle and namesake who died in March 1445: PRO, C139/117/4.
8. *CP*, ii. 242-43.

same man who from the later 1450s to the 1470s was periodically among the citizens electing the mayor and senior city officers.[9]

BRASUTOR, John the younger (*b*.c.1419), of Exeter

The brewer John Brasutor who lived in the Exeter parish of St. Mary Major in the southern city quarter was among the youngest of the witnesses examined in 1439. In 1428 he had been the victim of a violent attack by a gang led by one John Stoke.[10]

BUKKEBY, John

Bukkeby, of whom nothing is otherwise known, was among the men said to be associated with Roger Champernon* in early 1438.

BUTTE, William (*b*.c.1413), of Poughill, Devon

A tailor, Butte came from the parish of Poughill. He may have been the man of that name who was admitted to the freedom of Exeter in September 1451.[11]

CADE, -, ?of Poughill, Devon

Named as a servant of Nicholas Radford by one of the witnesses to the inquiry of 1439, Cade is otherwise obscure. It seems unlikely that he must be identified with the John Cade who was admitted to the freedom of Exeter in January 1425, having served his apprenticeship with the baker Vincent Hert*.[12]

CHAMPERNON, Roger (c.1411–61), of Bere Ferrers

Son and heir of Alexander Champernon and his wife Joan, one of the co-heiresses of Martin de Ferrers of Bere Ferrers, Roger represented the younger line of his old-established family. By the

---

9. Devon RO, Exeter mayor's court roll 15-18, 33-35, 37-39 Hen. VI, 1-11 Edw. IV.
10. Devon RO, Exeter mayor's court roll 7-8 Hen. VI, rot. 2d.
11. *Exeter Freemen* ed. Rowe and Jackson, p. 51.
12. *Exeter Freemen* ed Rowe and Jackson, p. 44.

successive marriages of his aunt Joan, Roger was closely related to several prominent Devon gentry families, numbering among his first cousins William Chuddelegh* and Sir Philip Courtenay*. In his youth Champernon fought in France, being present at the siege of Orleans in 1428. On his return to Devon he took his place in local administration, serving as sheriff of his native county in 1435–36, twice representing the shire in parliament, and receiving appointment to a string of *ad-hoc* commissions. In spite of his kinship with Sir Philip Courtenay and the latter's friend and patron William, Lord Bonville, Champernon was closely associated with Thomas Courtenay*, earl of Devon and his sons, and in the riotous mid 1450s on more than one occasion stood surety for their future good behaviour. In spite of this association, Champernon became a trusted supporter of the duke of York's administration that took power after the battle of Northampton in the summer of 1460. He was appointed to the shrievalty of Cornwall, and took his place on the south-western county benches. Although he had been married since before 1435, at his death just over a year later in mid November 1461 he left no children and was succeeded by his brother John.[13]

CHEKE (Chike), William (c.1409–52), of Bere Ferrers, Devon

Ordained acolyte in March 1422 and rising through the orders of subdeacon and deacon over the following two years, before being ordained to the priesthood in June 1424, Cheke spent the following two and a half decades as household chaplain to the Champernons of Bere Ferrers. He was serving Roger Champernon* in this capacity at the time of the inquiry of 1439, and two years later was among the executors of Roger's father, Alexander. On 1 July 1449 Cheke was installed as archpriest of Bere Ferrers, but held the benefice for less than three years before his early death.[14]

13. *The History of Parliament: The Commons, 1386–1421* ed. J.S. Roskell, Linda Clark and Carole Rawcliffe (4 vols., Stroud, 1993), ii. 573-4; H. Kleineke, 'Champernowne, Roger', in *The Commons 1422–61* ed. Clark.
14. *Reg. Lacy* ed. Hingeston-Randolph, i. 340, 369; *Reg. Lacy* ed. Dunstan, iii. 31; iv. 73, 83, 87, 90; PRO, CP40/734, rot. 263.

CHUDDELEGH (Chidelegh), Simon (*d*.1451), of Exeter

A junior scion of the Chuddeleghs of Ashton, Simon Chuddelegh was ordained acolyte in March 1422 and passed through the orders of subdeacon and deacon in September and December 1423, before being ordained to the priesthood in September 1424. He received his first benefice a year later in October 1425 when he was instituted as rector of the Exeter church of All Hallows on the Wall. He retained this benefice until January 1439, when he exchanged it for the parish of Holy Trinity. To this church he displayed some commitment, arranging for its rededication by the bishop in 1442. Further preferment followed in the summer of 1446, when Chuddelegh was collated to the prebend of Stowford in the collegiate church of Crediton. Throughout his career he was closely associated with the chapter of Exeter cathedral, acting as its proctor in a number of transactions, serving as clerk of its exchequer and as an executor of several of its leading members, such as the precentor Roger Bolter and the treasurer Michael Lercedekne. In 1449 Chuddelegh became rector of the largest of the Exeter parishes, St. Mary Major, in succession to John Boryngton*, but only held this parish for two years before his death in mid 1451.[15]

CHUDDELEGH (Chidelegh), William (*b*. bef. 1402) of Cornwood, Devon

The younger son of Sir James Chuddelegh of Ashton, Chuddelegh was through his mother, a daughter of Richard Champernon, not only the half-brother of the influential Sir Philip Courtenay* of Powderham, but also a first cousin of Roger Champernon*. He is frequently encountered as a witness to his more important relatives' property deeds, and not long before the inquiry of 1439 he had acted as proctor for the parishioners of Cornwood in a dispute with their rector over the mortuary dues payable by custom.[16]

15. *Reg. Lacy* ed. Hingeston-Randolph, i. 84, 249-50, 306, 339, 363-64; *Reg. Lacy* ed. Dunstan, ii. 260, 338, 343, 360; iii. 287, 307, 310; iv. 12-13, 29-30, 40, 73, 84, 85, 91; PRO, CP40/730, rot. 182; CP40/734, rot. 183.
16. Devon RO, Courtenay of Powderham (Moger) mss, D1508M/Moger/83; Seymour of Berry Pomeroy mss, 3799M-0/ET/7/6; *Reg. Lacy* ed. Dunstan, ii. 83, 85.

CLERK, Nicholas (*b*.c.1413), of Exeter

A weaver by trade, Clerk lived in the Exeter parish of St. Paul. He is not known to have been admitted to the city's franchise, or to have held civic office.

COBETHORN, Master John (*d*.1458), dean of Exeter

Evidently marked out for rapid advancement in the Church, Cobethorn (who then had only received the first tonsure) had Bishop Stafford's letters dimissory in January 1417, and was ordained to the priesthood eight months later. In January 1418 he was collated to his first benefice, the vicarage of Paignton, which he exchanged for the rectory of Cornish St. Ive that same May. In January 1419 he was admitted to a prebend at Exeter cathedral, and became president of the bishop's consistory court. On the death of Stephen Payne in May 1419, Master Roger Bolter, the precentor of Exeter cathedral was elected dean of Exeter, but refused the post. Two months later, the chapter chose in his stead Cobethorn, who became one of the cathedral's longest-serving deans, remaining at Exeter until his death in 1458.[17]

COK *alias* GOLDESMYTH, Tilman, of Exeter

According to Thomas Tremayne's version of events, Cok was the elderly goldsmith originally approached by Nicholas Radford* to repair the forged signet of Nicholas Tremayne. As his eye-sight was failing, Cok had declined the commission, and had instead referred the lawyer to his younger associate, Thomas Thorpe*.

17. *Fasti Ecclesiae Anglicanae 1300–1541* ed. H.P.F. King, B. Jones and J.M. Horn (12 vols., London, 1962–67), ix. 5, 48; *The Register of Edmund Stafford* ed. F.C. Hingeston-Randolph (London, 1886), pp. 62, 161, 169, 193, 202, 460; *Death and Memory in Medieval Exeter* ed. D. Lepine and N. Orme (Exeter, 2003), p. 58.

COLDWILLE, Nicholas (*b*.c.1415), of Weare and Cowick, Devon

At the time of the inquiry of 1439 Coldwille, otherwise obscure, was a member of the household of John Holand*.

COLLES, Master Walter (*d*.1453), of Exeter

Evidently designated for advancement in the church, Colles was presented to his first benefice, the rectory of Milton Damarel, by its patron, the earl of Devon, some four months before being ordained acolyte in September 1413. Over the course of subsequent years he passed into higher orders, becoming a deacon in September 1415 and achieving the priesthood in June 1416. He resigned Milton in the autumn of 1415 to become rector of the principal portion of the parish church of Tiverton. Courtenay patronage also secured him his next preferment, to the rectory of Crewkerne, in May 1422. When Earl Hugh died not long after leaving his son and heir a minor Colles was chosen alongside John Coppleston* to administrate the estates of the earldom of Devon during the minority. He soon also found employment by the new bishop of Exeter, Edmund Lacy, by the spring of 1421 served as official of his peculiar jurisdiction in Devon and subsequently received periodic appointment as Lacy's proctor in convocation and commissioner. Colles had been a canon of Exeter cathedral since before 1425 and became precentor following the death of Roger Bolter in April 1437. Between about 1434 and 1436 he also held in plurality the Devon rectory of Whitestone, and (having exchanged Crewkerne for the prebend of Heighes at Exeter in 1428 and resigned his portion of Tiverton about the time of his collation to the precentorship) he later added to his collection of benefices the rectory of Moretonhampstead and the prebend of Yatesbury at Salisbury cathedral, which he exchanged for a prebend at the collegiate church of Crantock in Cornwall in March 1453. In 1447 Colles acted as one of the proctors for the cathedral chapter in their dispute with the city authorities of Exeter, while in 1451 the bishop entrusted him with the custody of the Exeter hospital of St. John the Baptist during its vacancy. Colles's duties at Exeter allowed him little time to devote to his multiple benefices, and more than one of his successors complained of the dilapidation into which he had allowed his churches and their fittings to fall. He died just weeks later, having made his will the previous

December, and was succeeded as precentor by the future dean of Exeter, Master Henry Webber.[18]

COLMESTORRE, John (*b.*c.1379), of Tavistock, Devon

Variously described as a gentleman or franklin, Colmestorre was among the oldest witnesses examined at Exeter in 1439. According to his own evidence to the inquiry of 1439 he had been retained by Nicholas Tremayne* for over 30 years. Accused by Thomas Tremayne* of complicity with Nicholas Radford* and William Tremayne* in the alleged forgery of the title deeds to North Huish, Colmestorre certainly also possessed close prior links to Roger Champernon*.[19]

COOK, Thomas (*d.*1438), of Exeter

Cook, who served as one of the vicars choral of Exeter cathedral from about 1405, was preferred to the Exeter parish church of St. Kerrian in September 1408. He served this parish for nearly thirty years, but in the spring of 1438 he fell ill, whether of the plague that was then current in the region or another illness, is unclear. During his illness he was cared for by the weaver Henry Hornysbowe*, but died before mid-May, when his successor was instituted to St. Kerrian. He was buried in the cloister of Exeter cathedral.[20]

---

18. *Reg. Stafford* ed. Hingeston-Randolph, pp. 188, 214, 440, 452, 460; *Reg. Lacy* ed. Hingeston-Randolph, i. 86, 108, 211, 219, 221, 232-33, 376, 378; *Reg. Lacy* ed. Dunstan, i. 16, 81, 212, 239; ii. 60, 79, 353, 381, 394, 406; iii. 108-10, 174-75, 310; iv. 57-58; *The Register of Nicholas Bubwith, bishop of Bath and Wells, 1407–1424* ed. T.S. Holmes, (2 vols., London, 1914), ii. 1098; *The Register of John Stafford, bishop of Bath and Wells, 1425–1443* ed. T.S. Holmes (2 vols., London, 1915-16), i. 155; *Fasti*, iii. 98; ix. 7, 49; PRO, SC6/1118/7; Emden, *Oxford*, i. 465-66; *Death and Memory* ed. Lepine and Orme, p. 59.
19. PRO, CP40/715, rot. 247d; CP40/760, rot. 181.
20. *Reg. Stafford* ed. Hingeston-Randolph, p. 171; *Reg. Lacy* ed. Hingeston-Randolph, i. 234; *Death and Memory* ed. Lepine and Orme, p. 60; Devon RO, Exeter mayor's court roll 16-17 Hen. VI, rot. 45d; Exeter cathedral, Dean and Chapter mss, 2594/1, 2596/4; VC/3351, m. 5; *ex inf.* Nicholas Orme.

COPPE, William (*b.*c.1399), of Exeter

The Exeter panbeater William Coppe resided in the north-western city parish of St. Paul. He is not known to have held one of the senior civic offices, but did serve at least three terms as one of the aldermen of the northern city quarter from 1442 to 1445, 1446 to 1449 and 1450 to 1451.[21]

COPPLESTON, John (*d.*1458), of Copplestone in Colebrooke

One of the leading lawyers of his day, Coppleston found employment both under the Crown and with many leading landowners and religious houses throughout his native south-west. He served several terms as escheator of Devon and Cornwall, sat on the Devon county bench, was appointed to numerous *ad-hoc* commissions, and three times sat in parliament as knight of the shire for Devon. His private employers, most of whom drew upon his services as steward of their estates, included bishops Stafford and Lacy* of Exeter, William Bourgchier, Lord Fitzwaryn, Ralph Neville, earl of Westmorland, the prior of Plympton, the abbot of Buckland and the city authorities of Exeter. He served as one of the stewards of the estates of the earldom of Devon during the minority of Earl Thomas*, and after the earl had come of age entered his service as his receiver-general. Coppleston married the daughter of the wealthy Dartmouth merchant John Hawley, and at his death in 1458 was succeeded by Philip, the eldest of his three sons.[22]

COSYN, Thomas (*b.*c.1409), of Exeter

Few details of the career of the Exeter saddler Thomas Cosyn have been established. He evidently lived in the northern city quarter where he was periodically presented at the annual mayor's tourns for offences which included the trade in skins in suspicious places. Several of the fines so imposed were, however, cancelled by the city receiver as being impossible to levy.[23]

21. Devon RO, Exeter mayor's court rolls 21-30 Hen. VI.
22. *The Commons 1386–1421* ed. Roskell, Clark and Rawcliffe, ii. 651-3; H. Kleineke, 'Copplestone, John', in *The Commons 1422–61* ed. Clark.
23. Devon RO, Exeter receiver's account 19-20 Hen. VI; Exeter mayor's tourn roll 19 Hen. VI, rot. 1.

COTELER *alias* CARWITHAN, John (c.1399–?1467), of Exeter

One of the leading citizens of 15th-century Exeter, Coteler was admitted to the freedom in January 1417 in succession to his father, Stephen Coteler *alias* Carwithan. He first embarked on the civic *cursus honorum* in the autumn of 1420 when he was elected one of the city stewards. Two years later he served as receiver, and he later went on to hold the mayoralty three times, in 1436–37, 1442–43 and 1448–49. In the intervening years he served as a member of the council, held the wardenship of the Magdalene hospital and represented the city in five parliaments. Apparently a lawyer by profession, early in his career he found employment in the office of the sheriff of Devon at Exeter castle, and in 1426–27 served as undersheriff of the county. His counsel was, however, also valued by his neighbours: he frequently served as lieutenant to the mayor of Exeter, and as a constable and mayor of the staple.[24]

COULYNG, Richard, of Exeter

In 1438 Coulyng was parish clerk of the Exeter parish of St. Stephen, and lived with the 'stainer' Grene* in the parish of St. Mary Major.

COUNSEILL, Robert (*b.*c.1406), of Exeter

One of the lowest-ranking of the witnesses examined in 1439, Counseill was a mere labourer. He seems to have lived within the liberty of the priory of St. Nicholas, as fines and amercements that he had incurred periodically had to be respited on these grounds.[25]

COURTENAY, Sir Philip (1404–63), of Powderham

Heir to one of the junior cadet branches of the Courtenay earls of Devon, through his mother, a daughter of Sir Richard

---

24. H. Kleineke, 'Cutler *alias* Carwithan, John', in *The Commons 1422–61* ed. Clark; *The Commons 1386–1421* ed. Roskell, Clark and Rawcliffe, ii. 727-28; *Exeter Freemen* ed. Rowe and Jackson, p. 42.
25. Devon RO, Exeter receiver's account 17-18 Hen. VI.

Champernon of Modbury and the widow of Sir James Chuddelegh of Ashton, Courtenay was half-brother of William Chuddelegh* and first cousin of Roger Champernon*. In the 1430s he employed Nicholas Radford* as steward of his estates. During the lengthy minority of Thomas Courtenay*, earl of Devon, he became closely associated with the earl's eventual rival, Sir William, later Lord, Bonville. One of the leading landowners in the south-west he held a number of important offices under the Crown, served on frequent *ad-hoc* commissions and the county benches of Cornwall and Devon, and twice represented Devon in parliament. In 1455 Courtenay's friendship with Bonville made him a target for violent attacks by the earl of Devon's retainers. On 3 November, less than two weeks after the brutal murder of Nicholas Radford, an army of the earl's men on its way to Sir Philip's seat of Powderham was beaten back by Bonville's forces at Lympstone. On 15 November another comital force reached Powderham, laid siege to the fortified manor house and bombarded it for several hours. A month later, Courtenay's manor house at Cadleigh was ransacked by the earl of Devon's men. Sir Philip himself did however survive until 1463, when he was succeeded by William, the eldest of his seven sons by his wife Elizabeth, the daughter of Walter, Lord Hungerford.[26]

COURTENAY, Thomas (1414–58), earl of Devon.

Son and heir of Hugh Courtenay (*d*.1422), earl of Devon, and his wife, the countess Anne Talbot*, Earl Thomas was only eight years old at the time of his father's death. Although given livery of his estates in 1433 at the age of only eighteen, it was not until his mother's death in 1441 that the earl was able to recover the substantial share held by her in dower and by virtue of an entail. These included the family seat at Tiverton, which she shared with her second husband, John Botreaux*, forcing the young earl to establish himself at a secondary seat at Colcombe near Colyton. In the early stages of his career Courtenay assumed the place in society appropriate to his rank, fighting in the King's French wars and playing his part in regional government, but from the 1440s

26. H. Kleineke, 'Courtenay, Philip' in *The Commons 1422–61* ed. Clark.

his increasing rivalry with Sir William (later Lord) Bonville saw him increasingly become a force for disorder in the south-west. It was this rivalry and his consequent disaffection with Henry VI's administration that saw him participate in the duke of York's ill-judged expedition to Dartford in 1452 and ultimately led him to wage open war on his rival in 1454 and 1455, throwing the city of Exeter and its region into turmoil for some months. In October 1455 this campaign of score-settling saw the lawyer Nicholas Radford*, originally one of the earl's own counsellors, who had attached himself to closely to Bonville, murdered by a band of Courtenay retainers, led by Earl Thomas's son and heir. The following month, the earl's men laid siege to Powderham, the seat of Thomas Courtenay's own cousin, Sir Philip Courtenay*, a close friend and ally of Bonville's. The south-western civil war was eventually brought to an end by the intervention of the duke of York, who placed Thomas Courtenay under arrest. Although before too long the earl was able to secure his release, he died just two years later in early February 1458 at Abingdon abbey. He was succeeded by the eldest of his three sons by his wife, Margaret, the daughter of John Beaufort, marquess of Somerset, the murderer of Nicholas Radford.[27]

COURTEYS, Friar John (*b*.c.1403), ?of Exeter

Ordained acolyte in December 1416 and subdeacon in February 1418, the learned Dominican John Courteys probably served the early years of his vocation in his order's convent at Exeter, before moving to London and ultimately to Oxford, where he was regent master of the Dominican house by 1430. By 1444 he had further risen to become his order's provincial prior in England. He was periodically called upon to deliver important sermons: in the spring of 1438 he preached at the opening of the convocation of the province of Canterbury, and he delivered several sermons before King Henry VI.[28]

27. M. Cherry, 'Courtenay, Thomas, thirteenth earl of Devon', in *ODNB*, *sub nomine*.
28. Emden, *Oxford*, i. 504; *Reg. Lacy* ed. Dunstan, i. 309.

CROSSE, John (*b*.c.1399), of Exeter

A saddler, Crosse, who lived in the Exeter parish of St. Kerrian, was admitted to the freedom of the city in May 1429 on payment of the customary fine.[29]

DEVON, countess of, see TALBOT

DEVON, earl of, see COURTENAY

DREW, Benet (c.1389–1454), of Exeter

A notary, Drew was one of the more prominent citizens of mid-15th-century Exeter. Admitted to the freedom in December 1424, he was elected receiver in the autumn of 1436 and two years later assumed the mayoralty, which he held at the time of the inquiry of 1439. In 1437–38 and from 1439 to 1446 he served on the city council, but subsequently withdrew from public life. Alongside Simon Chuddelegh* and James Richard* he served as an executor of the former treasurer of Exeter cathedral, Michael Lercedekne. He may have come from a Cornish family, as he owned property in the parish of St. Probus. He probably died in the course of 1454, the year when he last received the allowance of bread and ale accorded to former mayors by the citizens of Exeter.[30]

DYBBE, John (*b*.c.1417), of Exeter

One of the lesser men among the witnesses examined in 1439, Dybbe, then resident in the Exeter parish of St. Paul, was a mere

29. *Exeter Freemen* ed. Rowe and Jackson, p. 47; Crosse must be distinguished from an older man who was admitted to the freedom in 1414, and between 1421 and 1434 went on to serve as bridge warden, city steward, receiver and member of the council of 12. This John Crosse may have died in about 1434, when he was last involved in the government of the city: *Exeter Freemen* ed. Rowe and Jackson, p. 40; Devon RO, Exeter mayor's courts rolls 9 Hen. V-13 Hen. VI.

30. *Exeter Freemen* ed. Rowe and Jackson, p. 44; PRO, C1/17/324; CP40/706, rot. 324; CP40/730, rot. 182; CP40/734, rot. 183; Devon RO, Exeter mayor's court rolls 15-31 Hen. VI; Exeter receiver's account 32-33 Hen. VI.

labourer. Said to be in his early twenties, he may have been the man who by the 1450s was trading in Exeter as a peddler or chapman, and who was later even styled a mercer. In December 1455 this latter man was among the retainers of Thomas Courtenay, earl of Devon, who participated in their patron's sacking of Lord Bonville's mansion at Shute.[31]

DYNHAM, Sir John (c.1407–1458), of Nutwell

The second wealthiest landowner in Devon after the Courtenay earl, with estates extending across four counties from Cornwall to Hampshire, Dynham was the son of Sir John Dynham (*d*.1428) of Kingskerswell, a man whose unlawful activities had excluded him from local office for much of his career. The younger Sir John substantially increased his wealth and standing by a highly advantageous marriage to Joan, daughter and sole heiress of Sir Richard Arches of Oving, Bucks., who brought him valuable holdings extending across Oxfordshire and Buckinghamshire. Although in 1444 Dynham quarrelled with the Exeter authorities, he successfully avoided being drawn into the far more acrimonious and violent dispute between Thomas Courtenay*, earl of Devon, and Lord Bonville. At his death in January 1458 he was succeeded by his eldest son John, who was later raised to a barony by Edward IV and appointed Lord Treasurer of England by Henry VII.[32]

DYRWILL, John (*b*. bef. 1399), of Tiverton, Devon

A cordwainer, Dyrwill, who is not otherwise heard of, was occasionally used as a messenger by Thomas Courtenay*, earl of Devon.

FELAWE, William (*d*.1438), of Exeter

The identity of the man of this name for whose soul the bells of the Exeter parish church of St. George were rung in the spring of 1438 has not been discovered, but he may have been a victim of

---

31. PRO, C67/42, m. 26; CP40/760, rot. 346d; KB27/787, rex rot. 4.
32. *CP*, iv. 377-78; Devon RO, Exeter receiver's account 22-23 Hen VI.

the plague then ravaging the region. He may have been the deacon to whom Bishop Lacy granted letters dimissory in 1421.[33]

FILHAM, Master William (*d*.1439), of Exeter

Educated at Oxford, where he was a fellow of Exeter College from 1404 to 1417, and rector of the same in 1407–8 and 1414–15, Filham was ordained to the priesthood in September 1410. Four years later the learned theologian was licensed to preach throughout the south-Devon deaneries of Plympton, Woodleigh and Totnes. He had to wait a further three years before collation to his first benefice, the deanery of the collegiate church at Crediton. Other preferment rapidly followed. In early 1419 he resigned his deanery to become rector of the parish of Stoke in Teignhead and a canon of Exeter cathedral, but he gave up his parish less than three months later when he was collated to the archdeaconry of Cornwall. He filled this busy administrative post which in effect saw him preside over the Cornish church for more than seventeen years, before serving a brief spell from September 1436 to his death in early 1439 as chancellor of the diocese of Exeter.[34]

FITZ, John (bef. 1411–1474), of Tavistock, Devon

A native of Tavistock, Fitz trained in the law at London's Lincoln's Inn, and served as a governor of the Inn from 1427 to 1430. He returned to the south-west to set up his professional practice in Tavistock, which he represented in Parliament in 1427, 1431 and 1432. Fitz appears to have survived until 1474, and was succeeded by his son John, who was admitted to the freedom of Exeter in 1476 and went on to serve as the corporation's attorney. A younger son, Roger Fitz, made his name as an important royal administrator in the south-west.[35]

33. *Reg. Lacy* ed. Dunstan, i. 9.
34. *Fasti*, ix. 9, 16, 48; *Reg. Stafford* ed. Hingeston-Randolph, pp. 160, 210, 461; *Reg. Lacy* ed. Dunstan, iv. 32-33; Emden, *Oxford*, ii. 735-36; *Death and Memory* ed. Lepine and Orme, p. 70.
35. H. Kleineke, 'Fitz, John', in *The Commons 1422-61* ed. Clark; *Exeter Freemen* ed. Rowe and Jackson, p. 59.

FOULER, John (*b.*c.1399), of Exeter

Ordained to the deaconate in early 1418, Fouler subsequently joined the ranks of the vicars choral of Exeter cathedral. In 1436, not long before the Exeter inquiry, he served as one of the executors of the chancellor of Exeter, Master John Orum, and six years later received preferment to the Cornish parish of St. Veryan which was in the gift of the dean and chapter. He left St. Veryan in 1447 to become sacrist of Glasney college, but resigned this latter benefice in 1451 and is not heard of thereafter.[36]

FYNKHAM, Alison, ?of Exeter

Fynkham, who is not otherwise heard of, was in 1438 engaged in litigation against John Person*.

GEFFREY, of Exeter

In 1438 parish clerk of the Exeter parish of St. Kerrian, Geffrey is not otherwise heard of.

GERMYN, Hugh (*d.*c.1476), of Exeter

A draper, Germyn was admitted to the freedom of Exeter in January 1428. Within a few years he took his place in city government and went on to become one of the most prominent citizens of the 15th century. He first held civic office as steward in 1434–35, was receiver at the time of the inquiry of 1439, and held that post again two years later in 1441–42. He held the mayoralty of Exeter no fewer than ten times between 1443 and 1475, and was a regular member of the city council in the intervening years. At the time of the inquiry of 1439 he resided in the High Street of Exeter in the parish of All Hallows Goldsmith Street.[37]

36. *Reg. Stafford* ed. Hingeston-Randolph, p. 453; *Reg. Lacy* ed. Hingeston-Randolph, i. 269, 315, 316, 363; *Reg. Lacy*, ed. Dunstan, iv. 23, 25; Devon RO, Exeter deeds, 5714M/T/13.

37. Devon RO, Exeter mayor's court rolls 13-18, 19-38 Hen. VI, 39 Hen. VI-13 Edw. IV, 14-16 Edw. IV; *Exeter Freemen* ed. Rowe and Jackson, p. 46; PRO, C1/53/200; C67/41, m. 31; C67/48, m. 12.

GLOUCESTER, Humphrey, duke of

Last surviving uncle and heir presumptive of Henry VI, at the time of the inquiry of 1439 Duke Humphrey had only recently relinquished his authority as Protector of England during his nephew's minority. His visit to Exeter in 1438 was remembered by a number of the witnesses examined a year later.

GOLDESMYTH, see COK

GRENE, -, of Exeter

Grene, whose craft was described as that of a 'stainer', lived in the Exeter parish of St. Mary Major.

GYLOT (Gylet), [John], of Exeter

A baker, Gylot was admitted to the freedom of Exeter in June 1415. Although he is not known to have held civic office himself, between 1425 and 1452 he was frequently among the citizens electing the mayor and other officers. He evidently resided in the southern city quarter, where the annual mayor's tourn periodically found him guilty of using unsealed measures.[38]

HAMMOND, Sir William (c.1403–67), of Tiverton, Devon

Ordained acolyte in February 1421, Hammond rapidly passed through the orders of subdeacon and deacon to the priesthood between March and June 1424. He had to wait for some years before acquiring his first benefice, the principal portion of the parish church of Tiverton, to which he was presented by his patron, Thomas Courtenay*, earl of Devon, in June 1437 after the death of the previous incumbent, Master Walter Colles*. He complained bitterly of the neglect which Colles had shown for the ornaments and books of his church, and may have been relieved to

---

38. *Exeter Freemen* ed. Rowe and Jackson, p. 41; Devon RO, Exeter mayor's court rolls 4-8, 9-11, 23-24, 27-28, 30-31 Hen. VI; Exeter mayor's tourn rolls 15 Hen. VI, rot. 1, 19 Hen. VI, rot. 1.

move three years later to the rectory of Aveton Giffard. In 1444 he added to this the rectory of Marwood, and held the two benefices in plurality until the summer of 1464, when he exchanged Aveton Giffard for the rectory of Berrynarbor. He died three years later, in the first days of 1467.[39]

HERT, Vincent (c.1399–?1463), of Exeter

The baker Vincent Hert was admitted to the freedom of Exeter in August 1411. He held civic office only infrequently, serving as one of the city stewards at the time of the inquiry in 1438–39, and again in 1454–55, and being elected to the city council in 1457–58 and 1460–61. He is last recorded among the citizens electing the mayor in the autumn of 1462, and may have died not long thereafter.[40]

HEWYSH, Oliver (*b.*c.1412) of Uplowman, Devon.

Styled a gentleman, the young Oliver Hewysh was a member of the household of Sir William Palton* at Uplowman. In 1440 he was one of the Palton men accused of an armed incursion into the earl of Somerset's manor of Sampford Peverell.[41]

HEYE, Thomas (c.1413–49), of Upcott, Devon

Rising rapidly through the orders of acolyte, deacon and subdeacon to the priesthood between March and June 1438, Heye was attached to the household of Nicholas Radford* that year. In December 1442 he was presented to the rectory of Poughill in succession to the recently resigned Robert Nywenhan*. He died young in the first half of 1449.[42]

39.   *Reg. Lacy* ed. Hingeston-Randolph, i. 193-94, 221, 257, 258, 290; *Reg. Lacy* ed. Dunstan, ii. 59; iv. 71b, 86, 88, 90; PRO, C67/40, m. 34; Devon RO, Chanter XII(i) (Reg. Neville), f. 22v; Chanter XII(ii) (Reg. Booth), ff. 7v, 8.
40.   Devon RO, Exeter mayor's court rolls 10 Hen. VI-3 Edw. IV; *Exeter Freemen* ed. Rowe and Jackson, p. 40.
41.   PRO, KB27/717, rex rot. 5.
42.   *Reg. Lacy* ed. Hingeston-Randolph, i. 277, 339; *Reg. Lacy* ed. Dunstan, iv. 165, 166, 168.

HOIGGE, John (c.1399/1404–1455), of Roseash, Devon

Hoigge, whose name was common in the late medieval south-west, is difficult to distinguish from a several contemporary namesakes. The early part of his career is obscure, but in January 1439, at the time of his installation as rector of Roseash, the benefice which he held at the time of the inquiry of 1439, he was said to be already beneficed elsewhere. He retained the rectory of Roseash until his death on 26 July 1455.[43]

HOLAND, John, of Exeter and Cowick, Devon

The Holands of Weare and Cowick were an important gentry family with close ties both to the Courtenay earls of Devon and among the citizens of Exeter. John Holand's probable brother, Richard Holand, was for many years retained as counsel by the city, while his son and heir, Thomas, became a trusted servant of Thomas Courtenay*, earl of Devon. John Holand himself had connexions to the Courtenays which were established by 1420 when both he and Richard fought in France in the retinue of Earl Hugh.[44]

HOLECOMBE, Roger (*b.*c.1393), of Exeter

A brewer, Holecombe lived in the Exeter parish of St. Mary le Steps. He was admitted to the freedom of the city in March 1428, and served as one of the aldermen of the western city quarter in 1432–33, 1435–36 and 1439–40.[45]

HOLME, Alan (*b.*c.1415), of Tiverton, Devon

Pantler to Thomas Courtenay, earl of Devon*, Holme remained in the Courtenay affinity into the 1450s. In 1451 he was among

---

43. *Reg. Lacy* ed. Hingeston-Randolph, i. 250, 298; *Reg. Lacy* ed. Dunstan, ii. 128-29; iii. 212.
44. *Reg. Lacy* ed. Dunstan, i. 258; PRO, CP40/779, rot. 327d; E101/49/34; E. Lega-Weekes, 'The Hollands of Bowhill in St. Thomas's, Exeter', *Devon & Cornwall Notes and Queries*, 18(7) (1935), 300-05.
45. *Exeter Freemen* ed. Rowe and Jackson, p. 46; Devon RO, Exeter mayor's court rolls 11-19 Hen. VI.

the comital retainers armed in the earl's campaign against Lord Bonville, and in 1455 he was the earl's bailiff of Coliton hundred. In the following year he was among the Courtenay retainers implicated in the murder of Nicholas Radford*.[46]

HORNYSBOWE, Henry (*b*.c.1409), of Exeter

The weaver Henry Hornysbowe was admitted to the freedom of Exeter in April 1424 after serving his apprenticeship with Roger Morehay. In the spring of 1438 he was caring for the sick rector of St. Kerrian, Exeter, Thomas Cook, and in 1439 he gave the Exeter commissioners evidence that painted Radford in an unfavourable light. He may thus have formed the association with Sir John Speke* which a year later saw him join Speke's force for the keeping of the sea.[47]

HUSSET (Hoset), John (or Janyn) (*b*.c.1414), of Exeter

The skinner John Husset resided in the Exeter parish of St. George. He was admitted to the freedom of the city in November 1432.[48]

ISAAK, Richard (*b*.c.1399) of Cruwys Morchard, Devon

A carpenter, Isaak was one of several witnesses from the parish of Cruwys Morchard.

KELVELEGH, John (*d*.?1448), of Exeter

Originating from the parish of Hennock, Kelvelegh was admitted to the freedom of Exeter in January 1426 after serving an eight-year apprenticeship with the mercer John Smerte. He intermittently served on the Exeter council between 1436 and 1445, and held the city's receivership in 1440–41. He probably resided in the parish of St. Petrock, where he served as churchwarden in 1444–45. By this date he may have been ailing, for in September 1444 he sued

46. PRO, CP40/779, rot. 183; CP40/780, rot. 153; KB27/786, rot. 118; KB9/15/1/24; C67/40, m. 25.
47. *Exeter Freemen* ed. Rowe and Jackson, p. 44; *CPR*, 1436–41, p. 419.
48. *Exeter Freemen* ed. Rowe and Jackson, p. 48; PRO, C67/40, m. 15.

out royal letters exempting him from office holding for the rest of his life, and he may have died not long after 1448, when his presence is last recorded at the mayoral elections at the guildhall. The following January Thomas Kelvelegh, probably his son, was admitted to the freedom of Exeter after having completed his apprenticeship under the tutelage of Kelvelegh and his wife, Juliana.[49]

KNOUDISTON, John, see TRACY

KYRTON, John (c.1409–61), of Exeter

Admitted to the freedom of Exeter on 9 May 1429 on payment of the customary fine, Kyrton rapidly became active in civic government, was elected steward in 1432–33 and receiver in 1435–36, and intermittently served as a member of the council from 1433 to his death in 1461. At times styled a merchant, he evidently had legal training for by the summer of 1437 he was one of the Devon county coroners and he retained this post until his death in 1461, when he was replaced by John Meryfeld. Probably as a result of his official duties he held no senior city office after 1435, although he was appointed one of the wardens of the Exe bridge in October 1454.[50]

LACY, Edmund (c.1370–1455), bishop of Exeter

Originally from Gloucester, Lacy was educated at Oxford and owed his preferment to the Lancastrian kings, particularly Henry V, whom he served as dean of the chapel royal from 1414 to 1417. In 1415 he accompanied Henry V to France and was present with

49. *Exeter Freemen* ed. Rowe and Jackson, pp. 45, 51; Devon RO, Exeter mayor's court rolls 14-27 Hen. VI; Exeter, St. Petrock's Parish, churchwardens' accounts, 2946A-99PW1, m. 17; *CPR*, 1441–6, p. 295.

50. *Exeter Freemen* ed. Rowe and Jackson, p. 47; Devon RO, Exeter mayor's court rolls 9 Hen. VI-1 Edw. IV; PRO, C67/39, m. 33; C67/40, m. 23; C242/12/1; C244/24/89d; C261/1/30; CP40/728, rot. 463; KB9/256/72-73; KB9/274/34; KB9/287/84-5; KB27/746, rex rot. 24; KB27/752, rex rot. 6d; KB27/774, rex rot. 1; KB145/6/16, 23; KB146/6/16/1.

the king to celebrate the victory at Agincourt on 25 October. Two years later he was elevated to the bishopric of Hereford, where he did not remain for long, being translated to the see of Exeter in 1420. He was a committed diocesan, preferring to spend his time in the south-west, rather than in attendance at the King's councils and parliaments at Westminster. He nevertheless played an important part in the government of his region, being frequently charged with tasks like the inquiry of 1439. It was during his episcopate that two drawn out quarrels between the citizens of Exeter and their bishop and the dean and chapter of his cathedral over the citizens' jurisdiction within the cathedral close and other ecclesiastical liberties within and without their gates came to a head. Even by 1435 Lacy may have been ailing, receiving that year an (undoubtedly welcome) exemption from attending council or parliament, on account of a long-standing disease of the shinbones which prevented him from riding, but he lived on for a further two decades, eventually dying in September 1455.[51]

LAURENCE, John (Jankyn), of Ottery St. Mary, Devon

A lawyer, Laurence found early employment with Edward Courtenay, earl of Devon, but also played his part in local administration as undersheriff of Devon. During the minority of Earl Thomas* Laurence served as a member of the council of the dowager countess Anne Talbot*, but was apparently also drawn into the circle of the earl's later rival, Sir William Bonville. Nevertheless, in 1438 he was playing host to both the earl and Roger Champernon* at his house near Ottery St. Mary. It is unclear whether it was his association with Champernon that prompted a brutal attack on him by Sir John Speke* which took place just weeks after the inquiry of 1439 had ended.[52]

---

51. *Reg. Lacy* ed. Dunstan, v, pp. vii-xi.
52. PRO, CP40/587, rot. 236; E13/128, rot. 16; JUST1/1531, rot. 20d; JUST1/1536 rot. 21; SC8/156/7798; C244/25/26; *CPR*, 1436–41, p. 370; M. Cherry, 'The Crown and Political Community in Devonshire, 1377–1461' (Univ. of Wales, Swansea, Ph.D. thesis, 1981), pp. 218, 227, 235, 253; *idem*, 'The Courtenay Earls of Devon: The Formation and Disintegration of a Late Medieval Aristocratic Affinity', *Southern History*, i (1979), 71-97, at p. 96.

LEGH, John (*b*.c.1409), of Exeter

If the age of thirty that Legh gave at the time of the inquiry of 1439 was correct, he was probably the man, then styled John Legh 'junior', who was admitted to the freedom of Exeter in September 1435, rather than the older namesake admitted in May 1429. As both men were skinners, their activities are difficult to distinguish, although it is known that the witness of 1439 lived in the north-western parish of All Hallows Goldsmith Street.[53]

LEGH, Robert (*b*.c.1379), of Exeter

Legh, styled a franklin at the time of the inquiry of 1439, was admitted to the freedom of Exeter in May 1429. He served as one of the wardens of the Exe bridge in 1431–32, but evidently did not rise to any greater prominence in the city.[54]

LOKIER, Walter (*b*.c.1409), of Exeter

The locksmith Walter Lokier, who lived in the parish of St. Olave, was admitted to the freedom of Exeter in August 1427. He is not known to have held senior city office, but did occasionally serve on presenting juries for the southern city quarter at the annual mayor's tourns. He seems to have supplemented the income of his craft by the brewing and sale of ale, and was frequently presented for breaches of the assize.[55]

LYNDE, [John], of Exeter

The identity of the man named Lynde whose house in the Exeter parish of St. Paul provided the setting for some of the attempts by William Tremayne* to bribe the witnesses appearing in the inquiry of 1439, cannot be established with absolute certainty. It

---

53. *Exeter Freemen* ed. Rowe and Jackson, pp. 46, 48.
54. Devon RO, Exeter MCR 10-11 Hen VI; *Exeter Freemen* ed. Rowe and Jackson, p. 46.
55. *Exeter Freemen* ed. Rowe and Jackson, p. 46; Devon RO, Exeter mayor's tourn rolls, 7 Hen. VI, rot. 2d; 13 Hen. VI, rot. 1d; 15 Hen. VI, rot. 1.

is possible that he was the John Lynde who had been appointed one of the city waits in 1434–35.[56]

MABBE, Henry (b.c.1409), ?of Colcombe, Devon

At the time of the inquiry of 1439, Mabbe was a yeoman in the service of Thomas Courtenay*, earl of Devon.

MAIOR, Master John (c.1392/99–1447) of Tiverton, Devon

Probably a trained medical man, Maior may have been the cleric who was ordained to the diaconate by the bishop of London in 1431 and who assumed the post of master of the Hospital of St. John at Hockliffe in Bedfordshire not long after. Maior was presented to the rectory of Cruwys Morchard in late October 1438, and resigned the benefice just over two years later on 23 December 1440. Two weeks earlier, Thomas Courtenay*, earl of Devon, in whose household he had apparently remained in the interim, presented him to the parish church of Alphington, where he remained rector until his death in the first half of 1447.[57]

MARTIN, Richard (d.1463), of Exeter

Having attained the orders of acolyte, subdeacon and deacon between June and September 1433, Martin was ordained to the priesthood on 18 September 1434. From the summer of 1433 he

56. Devon RO, Exeter mayor's court roll 13-14 Hen. VI, rot. 10d. It seems unlikely that the man in question was the clerk who in 1465 succeeded Master John Maior as rector of the Exeter parish church of St. Mary Steps: Devon RO, Chanter XII(ii) (Reg. Booth), ff. 3, 55v.

57. Emden, *Oxford*, ii. 1205; *Reg. Lacy* ed. Hingeston-Randolph, i. 237, 262, 325; *Reg. Lacy* ed. Dunstan, ii. 117, 119; iii. 296-99. There is some confusion over Maior's age: at the time of his presentation to Cruwys Morchard he was said to be forty-six and more, but at the time of the Exeter inquiry a few months later his age was recorded as forty. Maior must be distinguished from a contemporary namesake, a *grammatice magister* who served as rector of the Exeter parish church of St. Mary Steps from June 1454, and resigned the benefice in 1465 to enter the hospital of St. John the Baptist at Wells: *Reg. Lacy* ed. Hingeston-Randolph, i. 384; *Reg. Lacy* ed. Dunstan, v, p. xxv; Devon RO, Chanter XII (ii) (Reg. Booth), ff. 3, 55v.

served as one of the vicars choral of Exeter cathedral, where he had been a secondary from 1428. Nicholas Radford's* purported attempt to secure for him the living of St. Kerrian's, Exeter, in 1438 failed, and he continued as a member of the cathedral's minor clergy until 1459, when he was presented to the church of Branscombe, a benefice which he retained until his death in 1463.[58]

MICHELL, John (c.1389–?1456), of Exeter

Difficult to distinguish from several contemporary namesakes, at the time of the inquiry of 1439 Michell was one of the annuellars of Exeter cathedral. He was probably the man who attained the orders of subdeacon and deacon and the priesthood between December 1411 and 1412. He successively served as annuellar to a number of different cathedral chantries, and may also be identical with the man who acted as collector of the cathedral chapter's rents from about 1420. He may have died about the end of 1456, when the annuellarship of the Stafford chantry became vacant.[59]

MICHELL, William, ?of Tiverton, Devon

One of the servants of John Botreaux* charged with summoning Nicholas Radford to the comital seat in 1438, Michell is impossible to distinguish from his numerous namesakes. It seems unlikely that he must be identified with the most prominent of them, the Somerset gentleman William Michell of Wembdon, but he may have been the husbandman from Brixton who in 1443 was said to be in debt to the important Plympton Erle gentleman John Serle.[60]

58. *Reg. Lacy* ed. Dunstan, iv. 148, 150, 153; Devon RO, Chanter XII (i) (Reg. Neville), ff. 11, 20v; Exeter cathedral, Dean and Chapter mss, 2595/12, 2596/2 *ex inf*. Nicholas Orme. Martin must be distinguished from several contemporary namesakes.
59. *Reg. Stafford* ed. Hingeston-Randolph, pp. 442, 448, 463. Exeter cathedral, Dean and Chapter mss, 3550, ff. 129v, 155v; 2925/12; 2596/4; 5160 *ex inf*. Nicholas Orme. I am grateful to Prof. Orme for his comments on this man's career.
60. PRO, CP40/730, rot. 407.

lxviii The Exeter Depositions of 1439

MIREFELD, Walter (*d*.1454), of Exeter

A skinner, Mirefeld was admitted to the freedom of Exeter in January 1420. He first held civic office as one of the wardens of the Exe bridge in 1423–24, and served three terms as steward in 1426–27, 1431–32, and 1436–37. He may have resided in the parish of St. Petrock, where he served as churchwarden in 1442–43.[61] He died in August 1454, leaving his property in the High Street of Exeter to his wife, Agnes, for her life.[62]

MORTYMER, Thomas (*b*.c.1389), of Poughill, Devon

The otherwise obscure husbandman Mortymer was probably one of Nicholas Radford's* tenants at Poughill, and in the first half of 1438 was in attendance on the lawyer's wife at Exeter.

NAHILYN (Nahylyon), Richard (*b*.c.1389), of Exeter

The weaver Richard Nahilyn, who lived in the parish of St. Stephen, was admitted to the freedom of Exeter in September 1426. He is not known to have held city office himself, but occasionally stood surety for some of those elected.[63]

NELE, Richard (*b*.c.1416), of Tiverton, Devon

Serving as butler of Thomas Courtenay*, earl of Devon, at the time of the inquiry of 1439, Nele subsequently remained in Courtenay service and in early 1452 was part of the earl of Devon's force marching eastward to join the duke of York on his march to Dartford. By the mid 1460s he had set himself up as a merchant at Tiverton. His trading contacts included members of Exeter's commercial elite such as William At Wille*.[64]

61. Devon RO, Exeter, St. Petrock's Parish, churchwardens' accounts, 2946A-99PW1, m. 15.
62. Devon RO, Exeter mayor's court rolls 2-3, 5-6, 10-11, 15-16, 32-33 Hen VI.
63. *Exeter Freemen* ed. Rowe and Jackson, p. 45; Devon RO, Exeter mayor's court roll 17-18 Hen. VI, rot. 2d.
64. PRO, CP40/821, rot. 127d; KB9/15/1, 23; KB27/765, rex rot. 9; C67/40, m. 26.

NOREYS, John (*b*.c.1415), of Exeter

A skinner by trade, Noreys served as one of the aldermen of the northern quarter of Exeter from 1445 to 1447 and again between 1451 and 1453. A year later, he became porter of the city's north gate, a post which he held for at least five years until 1459.[65]

NORTON, Robert, of Exeter

Admitted to the freedom of Exeter in September 1423, Norton was a busy bell founder whose work was in demand throughout the south-west and beyond: apart from the Guernsey clients whom he had recently supplied at the time of the 1439 inquiry, and the Exeter parish church of Holy Trinity (where payments to him are recorded in 1428–29), he also cast a ring of bells for the parishioners of Plymtree, who complained of having been defrauded by him as to their true weight.[66]

NYWENHAM, Robert (c.1387–1457), of Poughill, Devon

Ordained to the deaconate in September 1418, at the time of the inquiry of 1439 Nywenham had only recently been instituted as rector of Poughill, a benefice which he acquired in February of that year, in succession to John Hoigge*. He resigned Poughill in late 1442, when he became vicar of Newton St. Cyres, retaining this latter benefice until his death in early 1457.[67]

ORYNGE *alias* TAILLOUR, Richard (c.1409–aft. 1472), of Exeter

According to a (probably spurious) tradition preserved by the 16th-century antiquary John Hooker, Orynge was descended from distinguished French stock and had come to Exeter from Anjou or Maine in the early years of Henry VI. Certainly, by the time of the inquiry of 1439 he was established as a tailor in the parish

---

65. Devon RO, Exeter mayor's court rolls 24-38 Hen. VI.
66. *Exeter Freemen* ed. Rowe and Jackson, p. 44; Devon RO, Parish of Holy Trinity, Exeter, churchwardens' accts., 1718A/add./PW2, rot. 10; PRO, C1/45/377; C241/222/30; C241/225/23; CP40/716, rot. 306d.
67. *Reg. Stafford* ed. Hingeston-Randolph, p. 456; *Reg. Lacy* ed. Hingeston-Randolph, i. 250, 277; Devon RO, Chanter XII (i) (Reg. Neville), f. 4v.

of St. George in the city centre. The date of his admission to the freedom is not recorded, but he was evidently a freeman by 1433 when he served as one of the city stewards. He went on to hold office as receiver in 1437–38 and was elected mayor of Exeter in 1454. In the intervening years he served as a member of the council, and continued to do so until 1471–72. From 1458 to 1461 he acted as keeper of the Maudeleyn leper hospital, and it is possible that he became infected, for according to another tradition recorded by Hooker he ended his days as one of the inmates of the hospital and was buried in its chapel.[68]

OWYNTYN, Walter (*b.*c.1409), of Colcombe, Devon

The otherwise obscure Owyntyn was serving as usher of the hall to Thomas Courtenay*, earl of Devon, at the time of the inquiry of 1439.

PALTON, Sir William (1379–1450), of Uplowman, Devon

A major landowner in Devon and Somerset, Palton was a younger son (but ultimate heir) of Sir Robert Palton of Paulton and his wife, Elizabeth, sister of William, 1st Lord Botreaux (and thus great-aunt of William, 3rd Lord Botreaux*. Palton was closely associated with the Courtenay earls of Devon, particularly with the dowager countess Anne Talbot*. He nevertheless played only a limited part in local government, holding only a single Devon shrievalty and serving short spells on the county benches of Devon and Somerset. In 1418 he served in France in the retinue of the duke of Exeter and may have formed a connexion with Henry V's brother, John, duke of Bedford. Palton married twice, firstly a daughter of the Somerset and Middlesex landowner Sir John Wroth, and secondly Anne (the Lady Palton referred to by several of the witnesses examined in 1439), probably a daughter of Sir Philip Courtenay (*d.*1406) of Powderham, and thus aunt of Sir Philip Courtenay*. She survived him and married

68. *Exeter Freemen* ed. Rowe and Jackson, p. 48; Devon RO, Exeter mayor's court rolls 14 Hen. VI-12 Edw. IV; *The Chronicle of Exeter 1205–1722* ed. T. Gray (Exeter, 2005), p. 46.

as her second husband the Devon esquire Richard Densill of Filleigh.[69]

PARKYN, William, of Exeter

First tonsured in September 1425, Parkyn was ordained acolyte six years later, and attained the deaconate and the priesthood in February and June 1433 respectively. He had to wait for some time before he acquired a benefice of his own, and was in the first instance attached as curate to Thomas Cook, the rector of the Exeter church of St. Kerrian.[70]

PAYNE, Thomas (*b.*c.1399), of Cruwys Morchard, Devon

A carpenter by trade, Payne, who in 1439 lived at Cruwys Morchard, must be distinguished from a man of that name who was admitted to the freedom of Exeter in 1429.[71]

PERSON, John (*b.*c.1414), of Exeter

At the time of the inquiry of 1439 the young skinner John Person was living in the household of Walter Mirefeld* in the Exeter parish of St. Petrock, perhaps as a journeyman rather than an apprentice, as his admission to the freedom of Exeter is not recorded. He may have been the 'John, servant of Walter Mirefeld' who was presented in the Exeter mayor's court in the autumn of 1438 for purportedly keeping Agnes, the former wife of John Costard, in a brothel. In 1440 Person was presented alongside Mirefeld for breaches of the assize of ale. He was apparently still connected with Mirefeld at the time of the latter's death, when he served as one of his executors.[72]

69. H. Kleineke, 'Palton, Sir William', in *The Commons 1422–61* ed. Clark; *Reg. Stafford* ed. Hingeston-Randolph, p. 217.
70. *Reg. Lacy* ed. Dunstan, iv. 98, 139, 144, 149.
71. *Exeter Freemen* ed. Rowe and Jackson, p. 47.
72. Devon RO, Exeter mayor's court rolls 17-18 Hen. VI, rot. 4d; 32-33 Hen. VI, rot. 48d; mayor's tourn roll 19 Hen. VI, rot. 1d.

POLBELLE, Thomas (*b.*c.1389), of Uplowman, Devon

Among the older witnesses examined in 1439 Polbelle was a yeoman of the household of the east-Devon knight, Sir William Palton*.[73]

POLYNG, Master John (*d.*1457/8), of Exeter

Polyng, the notary public who recorded and attested the testimony given at Exeter in 1439, found regular employment in the service of the diocesan clergy as a proctor or notary from the early 1430s. Before long, he also attracted the attention of the diocesan authorities and by 1449 he was serving as registrar of the bishop of Exeter's consistory court. He did not, however, enjoy universal popularity, being – like many other men of law – accused of sharp practices. So, for instance, one William Hoton, calling Polyng a 'chopchurch', claimed that the notary had prevented him from recovering a debt in the manor court of Moretonhampstead by producing forged letters of excommunication. Polyng was also employed by Thomas Courtenay*, earl of Devon, who in the summer of 1455 sued him for an account of the time when he had served as bailiff of the hundred of Haridge. He made his will in November 1456, and died within the following 15 months. He asked to be buried in the abbey church of Buckland, and among other bequests left his Exeter house known as 'The ynne of þe Taberd' to Exeter College, Oxford. Probate was granted in February 1458 and not long after his executors sought redress against the priest John Bouer, to whom Polyng had entrusted his possessions.[74]

POPHAM, Sir Stephen (c.1386–1444), of Popham, Hants

Popham came from an old Hampshire family with long traditions of service in local government. Probably educated at Winchester

73. PRO, KB27/715, rot. 44d.
74. *Reg. Lacy* ed. Dunstan, iii. 29, 69, 188; *Reg. Lacy* ed. Hingeston-Randolph, i. 148, 166, 199, 203, 240, 244, 245, 247, 349, 395; Emden, *Oxford*, iii. 1495; PRO, C1/17/86; C1/26/602; CP40/778, rot. 36; CP40/781, rot. 223d; Devon RO, Exeter deeds, 5714M/T/13.

College, he went on to distinguish himself on the battlefields of France, fighting in the duke of York's retinue at Agincourt. In keeping with this family tradition he twice served as sheriff of his native county, sat on the county bench, and represented Hampshire in five parliaments in the reigns of Henry V and Henry VI, as well as receiving appointment to numerous *ad-hoc* commissions, many of them concerned with the shipment of troops to France.[75]

PREWE, John (*b.*c.1417), of Tiverton, Devon

Serving as barber to Thomas Courtenay*, earl of Devon, at the time of the inquiry of 1439, Prewe probably came from a family of Courtenay tenants from Tiverton. No details of his career are known, but the man of this name who served as reeve of Tiverton in 1480–81 may have been either the former barber or a son or other kinsman.[76]

PYE, John (*b.*c.1409), of Colcombe, Devon

Pye, who at the time of the inquiry of 1439 was serving as wardrober with Thomas Courtenay*, earl of Devon, probably came from the same family as his older namesake who in 1422 was serving as reeve of the Courtenay manor of Aylesbeare.[77]

PYKE, John (*b.*c.1389), of Exeter

The skinner John Pyke probably lived in the southern quarter of the city, where he served as porter in 1431–32. It was probably he, rather than his namesake, a blacksmith, who was periodically presented at the annual major's tourn for selling ale in unsealed measures.[78]

75. *The Commons 1386–1421* ed. Roskell, Clark and Rawcliffe, iv. 116-17.
76. PRO, SC6/1118/4.
77. PRO, SC6/1118/6, rot. 1; SC6/1118/7.
78. Devon RO, Exeter mayor's court roll 10-21 Hen. VI, rot. 2d; Exeter mayor's tourn roll 19 Hen. VI, rot. 1.

PYPER, John (*b*.c.1379), of Exeter

Resident in the Exeter parish of St. Laurence, Pyper exercised the craft of a skinner. Although his admission to the freedom is not recorded, he may have been the same man who in 1440–41 served in the lesser city office of an alderman in the eastern quarter. That same year he was charged by the local gentleman John Reynell with his failure to return various household goods and items of silver plate, which had purportedly been delivered to him in 1422 at Basingstoke for safe keeping.[79]

RADFORD, Nicholas (*d*.1455), of Exeter and Upcott Barton, Devon

Party to the dispute which led to the inquiry of 1439, Radford was one of the leading lawyers of his day, certainly in his native south-west. From he early 1420s he not only established an extensive private practice, but also played a highly active part in local administration, sitting on the Devon bench from 1424, serving as escheator of Devon and Cornwall in 1435–36, and being appointed to numerous *ad-hoc* commissions, as well as twice sitting in parliament in 1421 and 1435. From 1423 to 1435, during the minority of Earl Thomas*, Radford served as joint steward (with John Coppleston*) of the estates of the earldom of Devon, and he subsequently maintained close connexions with both the earl and his widowed mother, the Dowager countess Anne Talbot*. Equally, he was well connected in Exeter, and in 1442 was chosen recorder of the city. Radford's clients did, however, also include Earl Thomas's great rival William, Lord Bonville, and it was probably in the context of their increasingly violent quarrel that he was brutally murdered on the night of 23 October 1455. Radford's daughter by his wife Thomasine*, who had married John Wolston*, had predeceased her parents, and his heir was consequently his distant kinsman John Radford of Oakford.[80]

79. PRO, CP40/716, rot. 307d; Devon RO, Exeter mayor's court roll 19-20 Hen. VI, rot. 2d.
80. *The Commons 1386–1421* ed. Roskell, Clark and Rawcliffe, iv. 168-70; H. Kleineke, 'Radford, Nicholas', in *The Commons 1422–61* ed. Clark.

RADFORD *née* WYKE, Thomasine, of Exeter and Upcott Barton, Devon

The daughter of the lawyer Roger Wyke of Bindon, and the wife of the lawyer Nicholas Radford*, Thomasine is most familiar as the ailing figure, bedridden since a riding accident in about 1453, whom her husband's murderers tipped out of bed on the night of 23 October 1455 before stealing the sheets along with all other moveable articles. The witnesses to the inquiry of 1439 describe a rather different, more resourceful, person who in the spring of 1438 took charge of the removal of her household from Corre Street into Northgate Street. Similarly, she is seen taking an equal part with her husband in entertaining guests, not least in the case of female visitors such as Lady Palton*.[81]

REE, John (*b.*c.1413), of Exeter

One of the lesser men examined by the commissioners of 1439, the otherwise obscure weaver John Ree resided in the Exeter parish of St. John the Bowe.

REE, Richard, of Exeter

A blacksmith, Ree, who resided in the Exeter parish of St. Laurence, was admitted to the freedom of the city in February 1437. He served as one of the two aldermen of the eastern city quarter in 1439–40, 1442–47, 1448–49, 1454–55, 1456–58 and 1460–61 and was a member of the council of 24 from 1450 to 1454, 1460–61 and 1467–68. He may have been a more substantial man than his craft suggests: in the early 1460s he was sued by one John Sterre for failing to return the sum of £20 in cash with which he had been entrusted. He died at some point in or after 1469–70, when he is last recorded among the citizen electing the civic officers.[82]

81. *The Commons 1386–1421* ed. Roskell, Clark and Rawcliffe, iv. 170.
82. Devon RO, Exeter mayor's court rolls 18 Hen. VI-10 Edw. IV; *Exeter Freemen* ed. Rowe and Jackson, p. 48; PRO, C1/31/36; C67/40, m. 15.

RICHARD, Sir James (*b*.c.1409), of Exeter

Probably the man who by 1436 was one of the vicars choral of Exeter cathedral, Richard, who was presented to the Exeter parish church of St. Olave in April 1437, did not attain major orders until more than a year later. He was ordained acolyte in June 1438, and subsequently passed the orders of subdeacon and deacon in the course of 1439, before attaining the priesthood in February 1440. He maintained close ties within the cathedral close, serving as executor to a number of canons, including the cathedral treasurer Master Michael Lercedekne and the chancellor, Master John Snetysham. In 1461 he received a bequest of six silver spoons and a volume of '*sermones parisienses dominicales*' from another canon, Richard Martin. He resigned from St. Olave in October 1446 to become vicar of Sidbury and retained this benefice until May 1462, when he was instituted to St. Thomas, Cowick.[83]

ROLAND, Richard (*b*.c.1413), of Exeter

At the time of the inquiry of 1439 Roland was a mere servant in the household of the weaver Richard Nahilyn* in the Exeter parish of St. Stephen.

SAMME, Walter (*b*.c.1413), of Exeter

A prominent Exeter tailor, Samme resided in the city parish of St. George. The date of his admission to the freedom is not recorded, but it must have occurred before 1445, when he first held civic office as one of the city stewards. He held this post a second time in 1448–49 and in the interim and subsequently served as a member of the city council. He probably died in or not long after 1457, when he is last recorded among the civic officers.[84]

83. *Reg. Lacy* ed. Hingeston-Randolph, i. 219-20, 310-11; *Reg. Lacy* ed. Dunstan, iv. 25, 37, 39, 40, 44, 167, 172, 173, 176; PRO, C1/16/265; C1/17/325; Devon RO, Chanter XII (i) (Reg. Neville), ff. 17, 137-38; Exeter deeds, 5714M/T/13. Richard must be distinguished from an older man who was ordained to the priesthood in 1422: *Reg. Lacy* ed. Dunstan, i. 46; iv. 75.
84. Devon RO, Exeter mayor's court rolls 24-36 Hen. VI; *Exeter Freemen* ed. Rowe and Jackson, p. 52; C67/39, m. 47.

SEYNTCLERE, [-], ?of Exeter or Tiverton, Devon

The identification of the man called Seyntclere to whom Nicholas Radford* wished to have the keys of his house delivered in Lent 1438 presents some problems. Ostensibly, the man in question, who was said by a witness not to have returned to Exeter until some time later, would seem not to have been a regular resident of the city. If so, he may have been the esquire John Seyntclere who by the early 1450s was a member of the household of Thomas Courtenay*, earl of Devon. There was, however, also an Exeter man, Henry Seyntclere, who in the summer of 1430 had inherited a house outside the East Gate of Exeter from his wife Cecily, the widow of Stephen Lucas.[85]

SHILLINGFORD, John (c.1389–1458), of Exeter

On account of his surviving correspondence with the city council one of the most widely known citizens of 15th-century Exeter, Shillingford was admitted to the freedom of the city in November 1418. A year later he embarked on more than 35 years in civic office, holding the receivership from 1419 to 1421, the mayoralty in 1428–29, 1444–45 and from 1446 to 1448, and in the most of the intervening and subsequent years until 1456 serving as a member of the city council. In addition, he served several terms as mayor or constable of the Exeter staple and represented the city in the parliaments of 1421, 1431 and 1433. His role in leading the city's fight against the cathedral chapter over the citizens' jurisdiction within the cathedral liberty is well documented, but it appears that Shillingford was a reluctant leader: from 1435 to 1444 he avoided public office altogether, and following his election as mayor in 1444 he initially refused to take the oath of office, and was only persuaded to assume his duties by the threat of a substantial fine.[86]

---

85. PRO, C67/40, m. 15; Devon RO, Exeter mayor's court roll 8-9 Hen. VI, rot. 36d.
86. *Exeter Freemen* ed. Rowe and Jackson, p. 42; Devon RO, Exeter mayor's court rolls 9 Hen. V-8 Hen. VI, 9-14, 23-29, 30-35 Hen. VI; *The Commons 1386–1421* ed. Roskell, Clark and Rawcliffe, iv. 361-62; H. Kleineke, 'Shillingford, John', in *The Commons 1422–61* ed. Clark; *Letters and Papers of John Shillingford* (London, Cam. Soc. n.s. ii, 1871), *passim*; *The Chronicle of Exeter* ed. Gray, p. 43.

SKYNNER, Thomas (*b*.c.1389), of Poughill, Devon

One of the older witnesses examined at Exeter in 1439, Skynner was a tailor from Poughill, who had at one time fostered two of the children of John Wolston*.

SKYNNER, see BENET

SMYTH, Pascowe (*b*.c.1412), of Exeter

Smyth, of whom nothing is otherwise heard, lived in the Exeter parish of St. Laurence.

SOMERHAY, John, of Stoke Pomeroy, Devon

A man of lowly status, Somerhay was a tenant of the wealthy Pomeroys of Berry Pomeroy. In 1436 he was employed by the feoffees of Cheriton Fitzpaine (who included Nicholas Radford*) to deliver seisin of the manor to Edward Pomeroy of Sandridge. Not long after, he was accused by a group of local landowners headed by John Holand* of having pastured his livestock on their land at Gatcombe.[87]

SPEKE, Sir John (*d*.1441), of Haywood in Wembworthy, Devon

Although Speke was the son and heir of a landed gentleman, through his mother Sibil, the sister of the Exeter recorder William Wynard, he had also inherited a legal family tradition. He consequently entered the law school of Lincoln's Inn, and by the end of the 1420s was of sufficient standing to serve as one of the Inn's governors. His life was nevertheless largely that of a landed gentleman. He increased his holdings substantially by marriage to an heiress, Joan, the daughter of John Keynes of Lashbrook, fought in France in the retinues of Sir Edward Courtenay (the earl of Devon's son) and Lord Maltravers in 1417 and 1428 and served as knight of the shire for his native Devon in 1437 and

---

87. Devon RO, Seymour of Berry Pomeroy mss, 3799M-0/ET/7/7; PRO, CP40/716, rot. 468d.

1439. He periodically provided legal counsel to his neighbours, the corporation of Exeter ranking among his regular clients, but within a few months of the inquiry of 1439 accepted a military commission for the keeping of the Channel and died not long after on 27 November 1441. His widow married an illegitimate kinsman of Roger Champernon's*, Hugh Champernon *alias* Rowe. Speke's son and heir died just three years after his father, and the next heir, Sir John's grandson John, was taken into the custody of the earl of Devon*.[88]

SPORIOUR, Richard (*b*.c.1399), of Exeter

A spurrier by trade, Richard lived in the Exeter parish of Holy Trinity. He does not appear to have entered the freedom of the city, unless he did so under another surname, and is not known to have held civic office. The on-going quarrel between the civic authorities and Bishop Lacy over their jurisdiction within the walls seems to have stood him in good stead, for the fines and amercements he incurred regularly had to be respited, as he resided within the bishop's liberty.[89]

STEPHYN, John (*b*.c.1376), of Exeter

One of the oldest witnesses examined at Exeter in 1439, Stephyn was a cordwainer and lived in Corre Street in the parish of All Hallows Goldsmith Street. He was admitted to the freedom of the city at an already advanced age in September 1423, but is not known to have held civic office.[90]

TAILLOUR, see ORYNGE

88. H. Kleineke, 'Speke, Sir John', in *The Commons 1422–61* ed. Clark; N. Orme, 'Sir John Speke and his Chapel in Exeter Cathedral', *Transactions of the Devonshire Association*, cxviii (1986), 25-41, pp. 25-28.
89. Devon RO, Exeter receiver's accounts 17-23 Hen. VI.
90. *Exeter Freemen* ed. Rowe and Jackson, p. 44. The cordwainer must be distinguished from a namesake, who served as one of Exeter's serjeants-at-mace between 1421 and 1434, and was admitted to the freedom in May 1429: *Exeter Freemen* ed. Rowe and Jackson, p. 46; Devon RO, Exeter mayor's court rolls, 9 Hen. V-13 Hen. VI.

TALBOT, Anne (*d*.1441), dowager countess of Devon

Daughter of Richard, Lord Talbot, and sister of the 'English Achilles', John Talbot, 1st earl of Shrewsbury, Anne married Hugh Courtenay, the future earl of Devon, in or by 1414, when their eldest son Thomas* was born. Earl Hugh died in 1422 at the age of just 33, and in 1433 his widow had licence to marry John Botreaux*.[91]

THORPE, Thomas (*b*.c.1405), of Exeter

The goldsmith Thomas Thorpe who resided in the parish of All Hallows Goldsmith Street, was the younger associate of Tilman Cok* to whom the older man had purportedly directed Nicholas Radford* in 1438 to have the forged signet of Nicholas Tremayne* repaired.

THRYNG, Master John (c.1409–84), of Exeter

Probably a kinsman of Andrew Thryng, four times steward of Exeter, John received apostolic license as a notary public in January 1430. By the time of the inquiry of 1439 he was procurator general of the bishop of Exeter's consistory court, but he found his principal employment in the service of the archdeacon of Barnstaple, Master John Waryn, as registrar of the archdeaconry. He continued in this post under Waryn's successors Richard Helyer and Michael Tregury, but in October 1452 succeeded his brother Richard as principal of Oxford's St. Mildred Hall. He held a number of university offices and in September 1453 took holy orders, being ordained acolyte and subdeacon on the same day. In September 1475 he was instituted to the Somerset rectory of Templecombe which he retained until his death in early 1484.[92]

TOKER, John (*b*.c.1409) of Poughill, Devon

No details of the career of Toker, a tucker who lived in the vicinity of Nicholas Radford's* home at Poughill have been discovered.

---

91. *CP*, iv. 326.
92. PRO, C67/39, m. 25; *Reg. Lacy* ed. Dunstan, ii. 221, 290, 314; iv. 45, 246; Emden, *Oxford*, iii. 1871; *CPL*, viii. 197.

TOTEWILL, William, of Lamerton, Devon

An associate of Nicholas Radford* and Roger Champernon* in the events leading up to the inquiry of 1439, Totewill was a west-Devon gentleman with landholdings at Lamerton and Plymouth. He had died by early 1447, when his widow, Joan, claimed a third of his holdings in dower.[93]

TRACY *alias* KNOUDISTON (Knowston), John (*b*.c.1415), of Tiverton, Devon

The earl of Devon's retainer John Tracy maintained his connexions with his master into the 1450s. He was part of the comital force during the earl's expedition of 1451–52, and also participated in Thomas Courtenay's violent exploits, including the murder of Nicholas Radford* in 1455.[94]

TREMAYLL, Nicholas (*b*.c.1419), of Colcombe, Devon

One of the youngest witnesses examined at Exeter in 1439, Tremayll was the earl of Devon's esquire. He may have died young, for nothing is known of his later fortunes: he appears to have played no part in Thomas Courtenay's violent exploits in the 1450s.

TREMAYNE, Nicholas (c.1367–1438), of Collacombe, Devon

Nicholas was the descendant of a junior branch of the originally Cornish Tremayne family which had established itself in Devon by the later years of Edward III's reign. His father had married Isabel, one of the heiresses to some of the estates of the Trenchard family of Collacombe. Nicholas further augmented his holdings by his marriage to one of the coheiresses of the Doddiscombe family, and succeeded in assembling an estate stretching over more than 1,000 acres. Before his death in 1438 he had made provision for the passage of his undivided estates to his elder son, Thomas*,

93. PRO, CP40/715; CP40/745, rot. 52d.
94. PRO, C67/40, m. 22; KB27/765, rex rot. 9; KB27/787, rex rot. 4; SC8/138/6864.

but it was his apparent failure to provide for his younger son, William* that led to a dispute between the brothers and ultimately the inquiry of 1439.[95]

TREMAYNE, Thomas (*d.*1481), of Collacombe in Lamerton

Son and heir of Nicholas Tremayne* of Collacombe, Thomas succeeded his father in the autumn of 1438, but almost immediately had to fend off the challenge to his possession of North Huish with which this volume is concerned. He rarely held public office, serving just once as a tax collector in his native county, and twice representing the borough of Tavistock in parliament. He married the daughter of Sir Thomas Carew of Ashwater, a granddaughter of Sir William Bonville of Shute, and thus first cousin to William, Lord Bonville. At his death he was succeeded by his second son, John, as his elder son had predeceased him.[96]

TREMAYNE, William, of Exeter

Younger son of Nicholas Tremayne* (perhaps by his second wife?). As a younger son with no expectations, Tremayne had married the daughter of an Exeter artisan, the skinner John Benet*, a match which does not appear to have given him entry into the city élite.

TRENEWITH, Nicholas (*b.*c.1415), of Exeter

The young skinner Nicholas Trenewith lived in the Exeter parish of St. Stephen. His name suggests Cornish roots, but no details of his connexion – if any – with the prominent gentry family of that name have been discovered. Nicholas himself never rose to prominence in Exeter, was not admitted to the freedom and apparently never held city office.

95. *CIPM*, xix. no. 452; CCR, 1405–9, pp. 301–2; *Inquisitions and Assessments relating to Feudal Aids* (6 vols., London, 1899–1920), i. 395, 445, 336, 486, 493; PRO, C1/7/73; C1/68/69; C140/80/34.
96. H. Kleineke, 'Tremayne, Thomas I', in *The Commons 1422–61* ed. Clark.

TURPYN, Geoffrey, of Exeter

Admitted to the freedom of Exeter in June 1432, Turpyn and his wife Cecily resided in the parish of St. Petrock, where he served as church warden in 1433–34.[97]

UNDY, William (*b.*c.1399), of Exeter

The glasier Undy lived in the Exeter parish of St. Martin. He is not known to have been admitted to the freedom of the city (unless under a different surname) and did not hold civic office. He was, however, of some standing among his neighbours, serving, for instance, as one of the feoffees of the lands of the local gentleman John Martyn.[98]

UPTON, William (c.1389–1451), of Exeter

The apothecary William Upton who lived in the Exeter parish of St. Martin, was admitted to the freedom of the city in December 1414. He rapidly rose to prominence among the citizens, being elected one of the stewards in 1423 and 1426, and holding the receivership in 1428–29. In the autumn of 1438, so John Wilscomb* claimed, Nicholas Radford* (who by then was renting the apothecary's house in Northgate Street) was thought to be promoting Upton's candidature for the mayoralty, but in the event he did not assume this office until two years later in 1440. In the intervening years and subsequently until his death in 1451 he served on the city council. Upton left a son, Roger, who had been godson of Robert Lingham, the rector of the parish church of St. Mary Major, but after his death his business may have been taken over by his former apprentice John Weston who entered the freedom at that time.[99]

97. *Exeter Freemen* ed. Rowe and Jackson, p. 48; Devon RO, Exeter mayor's court roll 18-19 Hen. VI, rot. 29d; St. Petrock's parish, churchwardens' accounts, 2946A-99/PW1, m. 7.
98. PRO, C1/72/78.
99. *Exeter Freemen* ed. Rowe and Jackson, pp. 41, 51; Devon RO, Exeter mayor's court rolls 4-30 Hen. VI; *Reg. Lacy* ed. Dunstan, iv. 14; *Death and Memory* ed. Lepine and Orme, p. 115; PRO, C1/19/191.

WARYN, Master John (c.1388–1442), of Exeter

Probably somewhat older than the records suggest, Waryn was ordained acolyte in December 1396, before passing rapidly throughout orders of subdeacon and deacon to the priesthood between December 1403 and March 1404. Already, in January 1401, he had been presented to the vicarage of Liskeard in Cornwall, which he exchanged in April 1413 for the rectory of Grittleton. Less than a year later, in January 1414, he exchanged Grittleton for the rectory of Cardinham, which he was to retain for a number of years. He was, however, destined for further promotion. Since September 1409 he had been registrar of Bishop Stafford's consistory court, and in July 1414 he had become dean of the collegiate church of Crantock. He resigned the deanery in May 1418, assuming instead a simple canonry at Crantock, which he surrendered in turn a year later in favour of a prebend at Exeter cathedral. By about this time he also held in plurality the rectory of Bondleigh, which he resigned in December 1420, accepting instead the rectory of Parkham, to which he was collated in April 1421. Further preferment came his way in late 1428 when he was collated to a prebend at the collegiate church of Crediton, and he reached the pinnacle of his career in August 1429, when he was made archdeacon of Barnstaple. By this date he had resigned his rectory of Cardinham, but in January 1438 he exchanged Parkham for the rectory of Shirwell, only to resign the latter little over a year later. He died before the end of July 1442 when his Exeter prebend was reassigned.[100]

WATTE, John (*b*.c.1409), of Exeter

A tailor resident in Exeter's Cory Lane (or Corre Street), Watte was admitted to the freedom of the city on 22 October 1431. He

---

100. *Reg. Stafford* ed. Hingeston-Randolph, pp. 153, 159, 160, 169, 184, 365, 443, 450, 458, 466; *Reg. Lacy* ed. Hingeston-Randolph, i. 5, 43, 114, 120, 247-48, 250, 272; *Fasti*, ix. 20, 48. Waryn must be distinguished from a number of contemporary namesakes, including the rector of Menheniot who died in 1426, and a vicar of West Anstey: *Reg. Stafford* ed. Hingeston-Randolph, p. 187; *Reg. Lacy* ed. Hingeston-Randolph, i. 8, 62, 91. Emden, *Oxford*, iii. 1996 conflates several men.

served as one of the city's serjeants-at-mace from 1439–46 and again from 1457–61.[101]

WELYWROUGHT, Thomas (*b*.c.1399), of Colcombe, Devon

Probably hailing from western Devon, Welywrought was serving as steward of the household of Thomas Courtenay*, earl of Devon, at the time of the inquiry of 1439. He also had connexions among the citizens of Exeter, who in 1433–34 rewarded him for unspecified services, perhaps in connexion with their long-running quarrel with the cathedral chapter. Although Welywrought remained in the earl's service into the 1450s and apparently participated in Courtenay's ill-fated march to Dartford in support of the duke of York in early 1452, he may subsequently have distanced himself somewhat from his increasingly erratic patron, and apparently took no part in the violence the latter orchestrated in 1455.[102]

WILFORD, Robert (bef. 1413–1476), of Exeter and Oxton, Devon

The Wilfords were a long-established and prominent Exeter family with close ties with the Courtenay earls of Devon. Wilford's grandfather and namesake had served as mayor of Exeter no fewer than thirteen times between 1373 and 1395, and his father, William, had held the office seven times and died in post in 1413. At the time, Robert had been a minor, but he eventually succeeded to his inheritance. In his youth, he served in the household of the precentor of Exeter cathedral, Roger Bolter, but subsequently broke with family tradition and established himself as a landed gentleman at Oxton in Kenton, playing no part in the government of his native city. He died in November 1476 and was succeeded by his son William.[103]

---

101. *Exeter Freemen* ed. Rowe and Jackson, p. 47; Devon RO, Exeter mayor's court rolls 18-25, 36-38 Hen VI, 39 Hen VI-1 Edw IV.

102. H. Kleineke, 'Welywrought, Thomas', *The Commons 1422–61* ed. Clark.

103. *The Commons 1386–1421* ed. Roskell, Clark and Rawcliffe, iv. 866-67; PRO, C47/7/6(1); C140/57/57; Devon RO, Exeter mayor's court roll 17-18 Edw. IV, rot. 7.

WILSCOMB, John, of Exeter

One of the lowest-ranking and most obscure of the witnesses of 1439, Wilscomb, a mere 'carrier of sacks', resided in the extramural parish of St. David to the north of Exeter.

WODE, Richard (*b.*c.1415), of Exeter

One of a number of tuckers among the witnesses examined in 1439, Wode lived in the extramural parish of St. Sidwell. He was probably the man who served as one of the city's serjeants at mace between 1445 and 1447.[104]

WODEWARD, Richard, of Exeter

Admitted to the freedom of Exeter in May 1422, the baker Wodeward lived towards the East Gate. In 1429 he was arrested and brought before the mayor and bailiffs charged with stirring up the men of his craft, and this misdemeanour may have precluded him from holding city office. From 1437 he was nevertheless regularly among the citizens electing the mayor and other officers. He may have died not long after the autumn of 1452, when he is last so recorded.[105]

WOLSTON, John (*b.*c.1389–1460) of Lezant, Cornw

Said to be aged over fifty at the time of the inquiry of 1439, Wolston was instituted to his first benefice, the Cornish rectory of St. Endellion in April 1414. Over the course of the following year he rapidly passed through the lower ecclesiastical orders, attaining the priesthood in February 1415. In 1416 he became rector of Bradford, and two years later, in May 1418, he was collated to the rectory of Lezant. Having served as parliamentary proxy for Bishop Lacy in 1437, he soon began to amass benefices in plurality. In January 1448 he took up one of the prebends at the royal chapel

---

104. Devon RO, Exeter mayor's courts rolls 24-26 Hen. VI.
105. *Exeter Freemen* ed. Rowe and Jackson, p. 43; Devon RO, Exeter mayor's court roll 7-8 Hen. VI, rot. 3d; mayors' court rolls 16-32 Hen. VI.

of Bosham, and in spite of a complaint early in his tenure over his (and the other canons') failure to provide for proper vicars to say the offices, apparently he retained this benefice until August 1455. In the interim, in February 1449, he had also taken up a prebend at the collegiate church of Crantock, which he held until his death in early 1460.[106]

WOLSTON, John (*d*.c.1449), of Upcott, Devon

A busy lawyer, although less prominent than Nicholas Radford*, whose daughter he married, Wolston was the son of the important duchy of Cornwall official Alfred Wolston. Unlike his father, John only rarely held Crown office, preferring instead to concentrate on his private practice. His clients included Thomas Courtenay*, earl of Devon, his mother, the dowager countess Anne Talbot* and his cousin Sir Philip Courtenay* of Powderham, as well as the communities of Barnstaple, Tavistock and Plymouth all of whom he represented in parliament.[107]

WYKE, Roger (*d*.c.1467) of Bindon in Axmouth

Son and heir of William Wyke of North Wyke (in South Tawton), Roger was the brother of Nicholas Radford's* wife, Thomasine*. Probably a lawyer like his brother-in-law (with whom he was occasionally associated in a professional capacity), Wyke served as undersheriff of Devon to Sir Thomas Brook in 1424–25. Like Radford, he formed a close association with the Courtenay earls of Devon, which in his case brought him into conflict with Earl Thomas's* great rival William, Lord Bonville. He was returned to Henry V's first parliament as a burgess for the Courtenay borough of Plympton Erle, and in 1454 found sureties in Chancery for

---

106.   *Reg. Stafford* ed. Hingeston-Randolph, pp. 184, 201, 427; *Reg. Lacy* ed. Hingeston-Randolph, i. 329, 337, 357, 396-97; *Reg. Lacy* ed. Dunstan, ii. 31; iii. 7, 45, 75, 86; *Death and Memory* ed. Lepine and Orme, p. 118; *Registrum Thome Bourgchier Cantuariensis archiepiscopi, A.D. 1454–1486* ed. F.R.H. Du Boulay (Canterbury and York Soc. 54, 1957), p. 195.
107.   H. Kleineke, 'Wolston, John', in *The Commons 1422–61* ed. Clark.

Earl Thomas. He married Joan Bingham, the widow of the local landowner Thomas Cayleway.[108]

WYKEHAM, John (*b.*c.1395) of Exeter

The hostler John Wykeham lived in the parish of St. Paul's in the northern city quarter, where the annual mayor's tourn periodically presented him for the use of unsealed measures in his trade.[109]

WYKIER, William (*b.*c.1409), of Coliton, Devon

At the time of the inquiry of 1439 Wykier was serving as constable of the earl of Devon's hundred of Coliton.

WYNTERBORN, Piers (*b.*c.1409) of Whitstone, Devon, and Exeter

Having passed through the orders of acolyte, subdeacon and deacon to the priesthood in just six months between December 1428 and May 1429, Wynterborn was presented to his first benefice, the rectory of Whitstone, in April 1437. He was to retain this for some thirty years, before exchanging it in September 1467 for the Exeter parish church of Holy Trinity by the south gate. Some years earlier, in December 1449, he had also acquired in plurality the position of a vicar choral at Exeter cathedral.[110]

YERLE, Philip (*b.*c.1409), of Exeter

Yerle who resided in the Exeter parish of St. Stephen practised the craft of a weaver, but evidently also traded in ale and perhaps wine, as he was periodically presented at the mayor's tourn of the southern quarter of Exeter for his breaches of the assize.[111]

108. *The Commons 1386–1421* ed. Roskell, Clark and Rawcliffe, iv. 919-20; PRO, CP40/660, rot. 318; JUST1/1540, rots. 52d, 55d; KB27/652, rex rot. 1.
109. Devon RO, Exeter mayor's tourn rolls, 15 Hen. VI, rot. 2; 19 Hen. VI, rot. 1.
110. *Reg. Lacy* ed. Hingeston-Randolph, i. 219; *Reg. Lacy* ed. Dunstan, ii. 39; iii. 54; iv. 121, 124, 126, 127; Devon RO, Chanter XII (ii) (Reg. Booth), f. 10.
111. Devon RO, Exeter mayor's tourn roll 12-13 Hen. VI, rot. 1d.

THE INQUIRY OF 1439

COMMISSION TO EDMUND LACY, BISHOP OF EXETER, JOHN COBETHORN, DEAN OF EXETER CATHEDRAL, AND WALTER COLLES, PRECENTOR OF EXETER CATHEDRAL, TO INQUIRE INTO CERTAIN ARTICLES (PRO, C66/443, m. 14d)

Rex Venerabili in Christo patri E[dmundo] eadem gracia Episcopo Exoniensis ac dilectis sibi in Christo Johanni Cobethorn, decano ecclesie cathedralis Beati Petri Exoniensis et Waltero Colles precentori eiusdem ecclesie salutem. Sciatis quod cum nuper comparentibus personaliter coram nobis in cancellaria nostra Thoma Tremayn, Nicholao Radeford et Rogero Champernon, prefatus Thomas allegauerit tunc ibidem certa grauamina et decepciones in quadam cedula nobis per ipsum adtunc ibidem exhibita specificata sibi per prefatos Nicholaum, et Rogerum certis diebus et locis in eadem cedula expressatis facta et perpetrata extitisse, ijdemque Nicholaus et Rogerus quandam cedulam eorum responsiones ad premissa continentem nobis adtunc ibidem similiter exhibuerint, asserentes se diebus et locis predictis per locorum distanciam non modicam personaliter non adesse ipsosque grauamina et decepciones predicta eidem Thome nullatenus fecisse siue perpetrasse, prout in cedulis predictis, quarum tenores vobis mittimus sub pede sigilli nostri, plenius apparet. Sicque cognicio veritatis congrua in hac parte ex causa varietatis huiusmodi que inter partes predictas intuitu premissorum exoritur et habetur nobis penitus occultatur. Nos igitur, certis de causis nos ad presens specialiter mouentibus super nuda et plena veritate in hac parte per vos informari volentes, assignauimus vos et duos vestrum ad inquirendum et ad vos melioribus viis et modis et mediis quibus sciueritis vel poteritis plenarie informandum de et super omnibus et singulis articulis versus prefatos Nicholaum et Rogerum per prefatum Thomam, vt premittitur, motis et obiectis, ac de et super responsionibus eorundem Nicholai et Rogeri ad articulos illos similiter, vt premittitur, factis et habitis et presertim de et super absencia dicti Nicholai diebus et locis supradictis et ad nos de toto facto vestro in hac parte cum presens mandatum nostrum in forma predicta fueritis executi in cancellariam nostram sub sigillis vestris vel vnius vestrum distincte et aperte certificandum. Et ideo vobis mandamus quod circa premissa diligenter intendatis ac ea faciatis et exequamini in forma predicta. Damus autem vniversis et singulis quorum interest in hac parte tenore presencium firmiter mandatis quod vobis vel duobus vestrum in execucione premissorum intendentes sint consulentes et obedientes in omnibus prout decet. In cuius etc. Teste Rege apud Westmonasterium xij die Marcij.

[*The King to the Venerable father in Christ E[dmund] by the grace of God bishop of Exeter and his welbeloved in Christ John Cobethorn, dean of the cathedral church of St Peter of Exeter and Walter Colles, precentor of the same church, greeting. Know that whereas of late, when Thomas Tremayne, Nicholas Radford and Roger Champernon came personally before us in our Chancery, the said Thomas alleged then and there certain grievances and deceptions specified in a certain schedule then and there exhibited by the same to us, done to him and perpetrated by the aforesaid Nicholas and Roger on certain days in certain places named in the same schedule, and the same Nicholas and Roger similarly then and there exhibited to us a certain schedule containing their answers to the premises, asserting that on the aforesaid days they were a considerable distance from the aforesaid places, nor did they perpetrate or inflict the aforesaid oppressions and deceptions upon the same Thomas, as appears more fully in the aforesaid schedules, the tenors of which we send you under the foot of our seal. And so a fitting knowledge of the truth in this part is thoroughly hidden from us because of such difference which has arisen and been had between the aforesaid parties in the examination of the premises. We therefore, desiring for certain causes specially moving us at present to be informed through you of the naked and full truth in this part, have assigned you and two of your number to inquire and to inform yourselves fully by the best ways and manners and means which you know and by which you are able, of and about all and singular articles moved and brought, as is aforesaid, by the aforesaid Thomas against the aforesaid Nicholas and Roger, and of and about the answers of the same Nicholas and Roger similarly given, as is aforesaid, to these articles, and especially of and about the absence of the said Nicholas on the abovesaid days and from the abovesaid places, and to certify to us separately and openly into our Chancery of your entire doing in that part when you shall have executed our present command in the aforesaid form under your seals or that of one of you. And so we order you that you attend diligently to the premises and carry out and execute them in the aforesaid form. We order, however, all and singular concerned in the matter by the tenor of these presents that they should be attendant, consulted and obedient to you or two of you in the execution of the premises in all things as is proper. In {witness} whereof etc. Witness the King at Westminster 12 March {1439}]*

EXAMINATION OF WITNESSES BROUGHT FOR THE PART OF THOMAS TREMAYNE (PRO, C4/49, NO. 31, rot. 1)

[m. 1]

Inquisicio et testium examinacio ex parte Thome Tremayn productorum coram venerabili patre et domino, domino Edmundo, Exoniensis Episcopo, Magistris Johanne Cobethorn, ecclesie cathedralis beati Petri Exoniensis Decano, necnon et Waltero Colles, dicte ecclesie Precentore, excellentissimi in Christo principis et domini nostri domini Henrici dei gracia Regis Anglie et Francie et domini Hibernie Commissarijs in hac parte sufficienter et legittime deputatis, habite et facte in domo Capitulari ecclesie cathedralis Exoniensis antedicte, capella beate Marie virginis et loco Consistoriali infra dictam ecclesiam situatis certis diebus, videlicet a primo die Mensis Aprilis Anno domini Millesimo quadringentesimo Tricesimo nono vsque in decimum diem Mensis Julij extunc proximo sequentem Indiccione secunda Pontificatus sanctissimi in Christo patris et domini nostri domini Eugenij divina providencia pape quarti anno nono.

[*Inquisition and examination of witnesses produced for the part of Thomas Tremayne before the venerable father and lord, the Lord Edmund, Bishop of Exeter, and Masters John Cobethorn, Dean of the cathedral church of St. Peter of Exeter, and Walter Colles, precentor of the said church, commissioners of the most excellent prince in Christ and our lord, the Lord Henry, by the grace of God King of England and France and Lord of Ireland, sufficiently and legitimately deputed in that part, taken and made in the chapter house of the aforesaid cathedral church of Exeter, the chapel of the Blessed Virgin Mary, and the consistorial place within the said church, on certain days, that is to say from 1 April 1439 to 10 July then next, in the second indiction, and the ninth year of the pontificate of the most holy father in Christ and our lord, the Lord Eugenius IV, by divine providence pope.*]

Walter Samme, taillour of the parissh of Seynt George of Excetre, the age of xxvj wynter and more, sworne, examyned and diligently required vppon alle the articles and matiers contened in the bill mynystrid bithe parties, that is to saye by Thomas Tremayn in that one partie and Nicholas Radeford and Roger Champernon in that other partie, to him worde bi worde oponly redde and declared, saith that he can no thing depose in the matier, save onely he saith that the Friday next afore Palme Sonday was twelmonth Richard Orynge, taillour, compleyned to this man sworne after none of the noyse of the bell of Seynt George, because that Roger Champernon and other were in his house disesid by the ryngyng of the bellis for the saule of William Felawe. Examyned if he sawe Roger Champernon the same Fryda [sic], he saith nay at his knowelege, but he saith the morne, that is to say the Satirday next folowyng after ix of the clok afore none and iij afternone the same day, the saide Walter sawe Roger Champernon take his hors atte the said Richarde Orynge is dore and ride, atte what certeyn houre he cannought depose. Otherwise ne more he cannought depose then he hath saide afore. He is nought corrupte by preyer ne price, as he saith.

John Watte yonger, taillour of Excetre, the age of xxx^ti wynter and more, sworne, examyned and diligently required vppon all the matiers and articlis contened in the bill mynystred and purposyd bi the parties aboue written, saith that he can no thing depose, savyng he saith that his duellyng place whiche he now duellith in and that tyme dede is and was the next house inhabite to the house whiche Nicholas Radeford dwellid in in Cory lane. Also wel axed and examyned what tyme the saide Nicholas remeued oute of the saide place in Cory lane, he saith as he supposith aboute Midlente Sonday he remeued into Northgate strete. Item examyned whether he knewe the forsaid Nicholas Radeford ete other sope in the saide place in Corylane after the saide tyme of Midlent Sonday, he saith he cannought depose. He saith that wel he wote that he was comyng and goyng thider til on the Friday next afore Palme Sonday was a twelmonth. Item the forsaid John saith that on Friday next afore Palme Sonday afore saide the forsaide Nicholas companyed with grete felawship come oute of the High strete of Exceter goyng into Cory lane before the house that this man now examyned dwellith in, and one of the saide company smote a blak dogge that was comyng and goyng to his house and he axid of one of Radefordis men who smote this dogge, whethir hit was Cade, othir his panter, he wote neuer. And he saide that hit was one of Champernon is men, and whiche Champernon hit was he wote neu*er*, and that tyme he se the saide Radeforde turne in to the saide house in Corylane where he duellid with the saide grete company. Item examyned ferther if he knewe eny of the saide company that went with Radeford, and he saith nay, saue onely Radefordis owen selfe and his owen men. Item of alle other thinges contened in the articlis he can ne thing els depose, savyng that he saith of his owen mocion that he is lever to say the sothe for one partie, than for that other, the cause whi he saith that Speke behight him good maistership and to saue him harmelesse. Other wise ne mor of the matier rehercid in the bill he cannought depose. He is nought corrupt by preyer ne price, as he saith.

John Stephyn, cordewayner of the parissh of Alle Halowe in the Goldesmythrewe of Exceter, the age of lxiij yeer and more, sworne, examyned and diligently required vppon alle the matiers and articlis rehercid in the bill mynystrid bi the parties, saith and deposes that on Friday next afore Palme Sonday was a twelmonth this man that is sworne sawe Roger Champernon, squyer, companyed with two felawis of his owen men and William Tremayn in his companye come oute of the High strete of Excetre into Cory Lane bitwixt vj and vij in the mo[rne tyde][1], and wente

---

1. MS damaged.

into the house that Nicholas Radeford was wonte to dwelle in, what they dede ther, he cannought say. Examyned if [he sawe][2] Nicholas Radeford or wiste that he was with in that house, he cannought say. He saith that he hath an house in Corylane that is his werke house, and ther in the same house that forsaid Friday he brewid, and bering in fursis oute of the strete, he sawe the forsaide Roger Champernon and William Tremayn passe into Nicholas Radefordis house, and ther spak with ham and bad ham good morne. And the said Champernon and William Tremayn turned ayein and said 'Good morne, John Stephyn.' Item he fortifieth his sayng by so moche that one of Champernon is men the saide day and tyme smote a blak dogge with his basillerd in Corylane. Item examyned if he can eny thing depose of the pretense dede and of all other matiers contened in the bill abouesaid, he saith he can none otherwise depose then he hath saide afore. Examyned if he were prayed by eny man to say eny other wise than the treuthe in the matier, he saith nay. He is nought corrupte, as he saith.

John Pyke, skynner of Exeter, the age of l[ti] wynter and more sworne, examyned and diligently required vppon all the matiers and articlis contened in the bill mynystred bi the parties, saith that on Friday next afore Palme Sonday was twelmonth betwixt vj and vij in the morne tyde the said John Pyke come oute of the castel bailly fro his gardyn by the toune wallis into Cory lane, beryng lekis in his arme, and ther in the same lane auentis John Stephyns warke house he mette with Nicholas Radeford and William Tremayn and other mo in his felaweship, what they were he wote never. And then the saide John Pyke helde oute his hande to William Tremayn to haue receyved money of him whiche he aught to him of lone. And the saide William Tremayn smote the lekis oute of his arme vnto the grounte and passid furth his way. And they all passid togedere in to the saide Nicholas place in Cory lane in his sight and knowelege. Item he saith that he sawe ther he wente by the saide toune walles a laborer in the saide Nicholas gardyne in Cory Lane. And when he come by the durre of the saide place of Nicholas Radeford he sawe hit stande opyn, by the whiche durre they entrid in as he hath afore deposid. Item examyned if he sawe eny of his neghtbouris being in the strete, he saith nay, saue

2. Damage to MS.

onely John Stephyn in his gardyne in Cory Lane, both the durris of his werkehouse beyng opyn. Item examyned if he sawe eny hounde smyten in said Corylane, he saith that he sawe none. Examyned also whether he sawe John Stephyn with oute in Corylane, he saith nay at that tyme. More ne othir wise cannought he depose in the saide matier rehercid in the bill. He is nought corrupte, as he saith.

Robert Counseill, laborer in gardyns, wallis and other labours, the age of xxxiij^{ti} wynter and more, sworne, examyned and diligently required vppon alle the matiers contened in the bill purposid bi the parties, saith that on Friday next afore Palme Sonday was a twelmonth the saide Robert Counseill, hired by one Robert Legh, citiseyn of Excetir, labored aboute makyng of the gardyn that longith to the place that Radeford dwellid in in Cory Lane, and ther that day betwixt vij and viij of the bell in the morne tyde he saw Radeford sittyng vnder a vyne in the saide gardyn lokyng in a roll, and sone after he sawe a man com for him, and he arose and wente with him. What man hit was that come for him, he wote never. Item examyned whi that he was hired to wirche in the gardyn by the saide Robert Legh, he saith be cause that the saide Robert Legh hired the same gardyn of Nicholas Radeford, as the saide Robert Legh saide to him. Ferthermore he saith that afterward the saide Nicholas was passid oute of the gardyn, he sawe two men com in to the saide gardyn to him and axid of him wher Radeford was, and he saide that he was gone oute of the gardyn in to what place he wist neuer, but he said here he was right now. Otherwise ne more can he nought depose in the matiers contened in the bill. He is nought corrupte, as he saith.

[m. 2]

John Ree, webber of the parissh of Seynt John the Bowe, the age of xxvj^{ti} wynter and more, sworne, examyned and diligentely required of alle the matier and articles contened in the bill mynystred bi the parties, saith that the Monday next after Mighelmasse day last passid the mayer of Exceter was chosen, and the morne vppon, that is to say the Tywesday, this man that is now examyned saith in vertu of his sacrament that he saw Nicholas Radeford in the High Strete of Exceter bitwixt the Yeldehal and the Brode Yeate bitwixt on of the bel and five after none, what houre in certeyn he remembrith him nought. Axid whether he had eny men with

him, and he saide that he had iij men with him and mo, and this
same man j sworn afterwarde the same day as he come fro the
Esteyeateward he mette Radeford on horsbak ridyng oute of the
toune, as he supposeth. Examyned more ou*er* of the Monday next
after Mighelmasse day last passid and of Thursday and Friday
next afore Palme Sonday was twelmonth, otherels the Thursday
next after my lord of Gloucter was passid Esteward fro Exceter,
whether he sawe Nicholas Radeford atte Exceter other no, he saith
he remembrith him nought. Item axid whether he can depose eny
other thing in this matier in gen*er*all other in speciall, and he saith
nay, savyng by othir men talis. He is nought corrupte, as he saith.

    Henry Hornysbowe, webber of Excetre, xxx^ti wynter of age
and more, sworne, examyned and diligently required of all the
matiers and articlis contened in the bill mynystrid bi the parties,
saith bi the vertu of his sacrament that on Friday next afore Palme
Sonday was twelmonth betwixt viij and ix afore none Nicholas
Radeford come into the close of Exceter and into the comon place
of the vicaries callid Calendrishay, to visite one of the vicaries
callid Sir Thomas Cook, than beyng seke, p*ar*son at that tyme of
Seynt Kyeran chirche of Exceter, of wham this man now sworne
had kepyng in his sekenes, and tretid him for to resigne his said
chirche til one Sir Richard Martyn, as the saide Sir Thomas Cook
tolde him afterward. And then duryng their communicacion come
ther a man and callede atte the durre and axed whether Radeford
wer ther in, and this man now sworne answered and said yee.
And then Radeford herd tham speke, and axid if hit were his
cosyn Champernon is man, and he said yee. And then Nicholas
Radeford bad that Champernon shulde go to Seynt Petris chirche
and abide him ther. And anone furth with he toke his leue and
departid thens. Examyned who was ther atte that tyme also wel
as he, he saith ther was the person that was seke, Radeford, this
man sworne and one Geffrey, clerk of the parissh chirche of Seynt
Kyerans. Also in fortifiyng of his tale he saith that the saide p*ar*son
sende the morne after to Radeford two canon loves. Also he saith
that a prest callid Sir William Parkyn that now syngeth for the
saide p*ar*son tolde this man in his owen house that the saide
p*ar*son tolde him this matier in his chambre the Monday next
after. Forthermore he saith that the mayer of Exceter was chosyn
the Monday next after Mighelmasday last passid, and the morne
vppon this man sworne saith that William Tremayn come to his

hous in Northgate strete in the mornyng and axid him if he sawe Radeford, and he said nay and said to the said William 'Go to his house and I trowe thow shalte fynde him ther.' He wente, as this man now sworne counselid him, and fonde his durre sparred and abode ther a litel tyme, and then come ayen and abode with this man sworne in his house. And this man wente oute in to the strete and sawe Nicholas Radeford come oute of his house in Northgate strete and a russet cloke caste ou*er* his hede, be cause the weder was rayne, goyng into the High Strete ward aboute vj or seven of the clok in the mornyng, as he supposith. And this man saide furth with to William Tremayn 'Yonder goth Radford, go after him.' And as tochyng all other thingis contened in the bill of the articles, he can no ferther depose then he hath saide before. He is nough corrupte, as he saith.

Philip Yerle, wever of the parissh of Seynt Stephen is of Excetre, the age of xxx^ti wynter and more sworn, examyned and diligently required of all the matiers and articlis rehercid in the bill mynystrid bi the parties, saith that on Friday next afore Palme Sonday was a twelmonth he, comyng oute of his house nygh to Cory Lane, saith by the vertu of his sacrament that he sawe Nicholas Radeford betwixt vij and viij in the mornyng passe oute of the high strete into Cory Lane, whether he passed in to his place in the sade Cory lane other no, he wote never. Inquered ferthermore how he knowith that hit was that Friday next afore Palme Sonday was twelmonth, he saith the cause is that he had the key of the chirche that day in his kepyng, and anone after the clerk of the said chirche fetchid the key of the chirche for to make palme. Inquired ferthermore who was the clerk that tyme, and he saith that is name is Richard Coulyng dwellyng with one Grene, stayno*ur* of the parissh of Seynt Mary the more. Inquired what men wente with Radeford that tyme, he saith two men, whether they were his owen men other no, he wote neu*er*. Item examyned how Thomas Tremayn come to knowelege that this man now sworne shulde be to him necessary witnesse, he saith bi that he shall declare here after in his examynacion. Inquired ferther in this matier what he can say, he saith that on Tywesday, the morne next vppon the mayer was chosyn, that was the morne sevenyght after Mighelmasse day that last was, he come to Nicholas Radeford afore one Hugh Germyn is durre in the High Strete of Exceter in the parissh of Alle Halowe in the goldesmyth rewe, and William Tremayn with him. And for

as moche as they were bothe boundyn to the pees that one to
that other sute, they prayed by comon assente to the said Nicholas
Radeford, justice of pees, that if hit liked him to graunte ham
a relece of their surte of pees that they were boundyn in eyther
to other, sayng that they were accordid of all their debatis. And
the forsaide Nicholas said that they shuld sue to his clerk and hit
shuld be done all redy. Item inquired whether he haue receyved
eny money in Thomas Tremaynes party for to depose in this
matier, he saith nay, saue onely for the tyme that he was lette of
his occupacion he was promysed forto haue ben rewardid. He is
nought corrupt, as he saith.

Richard Roland, seruant of Richard Nahilyn, wever, of the
parissh of Seynt Stephyn of Exceter, xxvj^{ti} wynter of age and more,
sworne, examyned and diligently required vppon alle the articles
and matiers contened in the bill mynystrid by the parties, he saith
that he can no thing say, savyng onely that the Monday next after
Mighelmasseday that last was the mayer of Exceter was chosyn,
and the morne vppon, that is to say the Tywesday, he saith bi the
vertu of his sacramente that he sawe Nicholas Radeford betwixt
iiij and v after none ryde in the High Strete of Exceter toward
the Est yeate and iij men on horsbak with him and a man on fote
talkyng with the saide Nicholas Radeford, beryng his hode on his
shulder. Inquired whether he knewe the men that were with the
saide Nicholas at that tyme, he saith nay. Item inquired wherby he
knowith that Tywesday afore deposid afore a nother day, he saith
bi that that he came fro a place callede Monkyn Sele wher he was
born the Sonday next afore that the saide mayer was chosyn, and
the Tywesday next after he sawe the saide Nicholas, as he hath
afore deposid. He is nought corrupte, as he saith.

Richard Spriour of the parissh of Seynt Trinite of Exceter, xl
wynter of age, sworne, examyned and diligently required of all
the matier contened in the bill declarid to him in Englissh as hit is
writon in the said bill, he saith that he can no thing depose in the
saide matiers rehersid in the said bill, saue onely that he come to
Richard Taillouris house in the parissh of Seynt George of Exceter
the Friday next afore Palme Sonday was twelmonth afore mete
and brought with him ij pair of sporis, and ther he fonde Roger
Champernon in a chamber with in that place and spake with him.
And the said Champernon handelid the said sporis and said that
they were nought for his weryng, and so he departid fro him. And

furth with two of the saide Champernon is men changid their
olde sporis with him for newe sporis and receyued of that one vj
d. and of that other viij d. Ferther examyned what causith him to
remembre of that day in certeyn afore a nother day, he saithe be
cause that William Tremayn come to his house in Trinite parisshe
ther as he dwellith now, and had of him a payre of sporis newe
blakkid with white ruwellis. Axed if he can eny otherwise depose
in this matiers, and he saith nay, other wise than he hath afor
deposid. He is nought corrupte, as he saith.

[m. 3]

Thomas Cosyn, sadeler of Exceter, xxx^ti yeer of age and more,
sworne, examyned and diligently required of alle the matiers
contened in the bill mynystred by the parties, he saith that he
can no thing depose in that matier, save only that he saith that
on Monday next after Mighel masse day last was the mayer of
Exceter was chosen, and the morne next after, that is to say the
Tywesday, this man now sworn beyng in his shop in Waterbear
strete sawe Nicholas Radeford comyng furth by his saide shop oute
of Northgate Strete passyng in to Paule Strete toward Seynt Paule
chirche, a russet cloke caste on his hede and William Tremayn
ledyng him by the arme, and the said Nicholas is clerk folowyng
him, betwixt viij and ix of the bel afore none. And the saide
William Tremayn said to this man sworne whan he come afore
his shop 'Is my sadell a redie?' And he answerid and saide that
hit shulde be redie that same day. And wan they were passid this
man sworne lokid oute of his shop and saide to John Batyn, toker,
his neghboure, 'Lo, this gosehede William Tremayn is becomyn
Radefordis felawe!' And the saide John Batyn saide 'Now he shall
thrive'. He is nought corrupte, as he saith.

   John Batyn, toker of the parissh of Seynt Pancrace, xxx^ti wynter
of age and more, sworne, examyned and diligently required vppon
all the matiers and articlis contened in the bill mynystrid bi the
parties, he saith that he can no thing depose in that matier, saue
onely that he saith that on Monday next after Mighelmasse day
last was the mayer of Exceter was chosen and the morne next after,
that is to say the Tywesday, this man sworne beyng in his shop in
Waterbere strete sawe Nicholas Radeford come furth by his shop
oute of Northgate Strete passyng oute of Paule Strete toward Seynt

Paule chirche, and a russet cloke caste ouer his hede and William Tremayn ledyng hym by the arme, and the saide Nicholas clerk folowyng ham betwixt viij and ix of the clok afore none, and herde wher that William Tremayn axid of Thomas Cosyn Sadeler his neghbour whether his sadill were redie. What answer he yaf to the saide William, he wote neu*er*. And whan the said Radeford and William Tremayn were passid Thomas Cosyn saide to this man sworne 'Lo, this gosehede is become Radeforde is felawe!' And then he answerd and saide that he that gothe with his better may lerne som good. Ferthermore axid what maner wedir hit was that day, he answerd and said that hit was moyse wedir. He is nought corrupte, as he saith.

Walter Lokier of Exceter, lokier, xxx^ti wynter of age and more, dwellyng in Seynt Olauys parissh, sworne, examyned and diligently required vppon alle the matiers and articlis rehercid in the bill mynystrid bi the parties, saith that he can no thing depose in the saide matiers and articlis, save he saith that on Wandisday next a fore Passion Sonday was twelmonth Nicholas Radefordis wife sente for this man sworne to make hire a lacche of iren and to amende a springe lok in Upton is place in North gate strete wher the saide Nicholas dwellid at that tyme, and thider he come that same day and saide hit shulde be done, and ther he sawe the saide Nicholas Radeforde in his p*ar*lour redyng in a boke that same Wandisday, in so moche that the said Nicholas desirid that this man sworne shulde make him a lok for the hinder dore of his halle atte Uppecote, and the saide Nicholas saide to him that he wist never what man*er* lok wer best for that durre, be cause the durre was made of so thik plankis, and this man sworne saide that he wolde make a lok and the same durre shulde serue for the stok and hit shuld be redy ayenst Wandisday next after, the whiche Wandisday was next afore Palme Sonday was twelmonth, and that Wandisday ther come no man after that lok, no the morne after, til after Palme Sonday, what day in certeyn he cannought depose. Ferthermore axed whether he haue eny thing receyued for to depose in this matier, he saith nay, saue onely that he saith that he hath bene in company wher that hit was comonyd amongis peple of the p*re*sence and absence of Nicholas Radeford, wher that som saide that they sawe him in one place, an som saide in a nother. Forthermore he saith bi the vertu of his othe that he sawe Roger Champernon in Seynt Petris chirche hay of Exceter the Friday next

afore Palme Sonday was twelmonth betwixt ij of the bel and iiij
after none betwixt Seynt Mary chirche and the litil stile goyng
towardis Seynt Petris chirche and ij or iij men folowyng him, and
the cause was that he sawe him ther atte that tyme, for he had
be atte Maister William Filham is house and had sette a lok on
a durre ther and was goyng hamward. Examyned how he knewe
that hit was Roger Champernon, he saith cause was principally
for as moche as he had be shiref the next yeer afore. He is nought
corrupte, as he saith.

Roger Holecombe, brewer of the parissh of Seynt Marie the
stappis of Exceter, xlvj wynter of age and more, sworn, examyned
and diligently required vppon alle the articles and matiers
contened in the bill mynystred bi the parties aboue nevened, saith
that aboute myd lente was twelmonth he come to Robert Norton,
belmaker of Exceter, whiche aught him a certeyn money for ale,
and the said Robert said to him that he shulde make iij bellis into
Garnesey and also sone as he had receyved money for the same
bellis, he shulde be payed for his ale, for he saide that ther was a
Garnesey man atte William atte Wille atte hoste that shulde make
payment for the bellis, and so he abode by this answer at that tyme
til on Friday next afore Palme Sonday was twelmonth, whiche
Friday this man sworne herde in his house a knyll ryngyng atte
Seynt George chirche atte iij of the clok after none, and also sone
as the knyll was sesid he wente vp in to the toune to one Keluelegh
merceris shop, for to bie certeyn spicery. And whan he had done,
he passid hamward by one Richard Taillouris house betwixt iij
and iiij of the clok after none, wher and what tyme he sawe Roger
Champernon go into the saide Richard Taillours house and iij men
folowyng him. Examyned whether he was botid and sporid other
no, he said that he was hosid and shod. Otherwise cannought say
ne more depose in the matier contenid in the bill. He is nought
corrupte by price ne preyer, as he saith.

Paschow Smyth of the parissh of Seynt Laurence of Exceter, xxvij
wynter of age and more, sworn, examyned and diligently required
of all the matiers and articlis contened in the bill mynystred bi the
parties, saith that on Monday next after Mighelmasday last was
the mair of Exceter was chosyn, and the morne next after, that is
to say the Tywesday, he saw Nicholas Radeford ride in the High
Strete of Exceter toward the Estyeate betwixt one and thre of the
belle after none with iij hors and a man goyng on fote with him

bare hede and helde his honde on his bridell. Examyned whether he can eny thing in gen*e*ral or in speciall say in the matier betwixt the said parties, he saith none other wise then he hath saide afore. He is nought corrupte, as he saith.

John Dybbe, laborer of the parissh of Seynt Paule of Exceter, xxij^{ti} wynter of age, sworne, examyned and diligently required vppon all the matiers and articles contened in the bill mynystrid by the parties, saith that he can no thing depose, saue onely that he saith of his verrey knowelege that on Friday next afore Palme Sonday was twelmonth he sawe Roger Champernon in the High Strete of Exceter ayenst Carfox with moche peple folowyng him. Examyned how he remembrith him that hit was that Friday more than a nother, he saith he was shriven on Satirday next afore Palme Sonday and nought before, and the Friday next before he sawe Champernon as he hath deposid before, and that causith him to be so remembrid. Examyned ferthermore if he can eny othir thing depose, he saith that on Tywesday next after Mighelmasse day was twelmonth he saw Nicholas Radeford in the High Strete of Exceter betwixt Alhalowe chirche and Richard Wodewardis place toward the Est yeate, and ther wente with him William Tremayn and his clerk, and a cloke on his hede. He is nought corrupte, as he saith.

[m. 4]

John Brasutor yonger, brasutor of the parissh of Seynt Mary the more of the cite of Exceter, xx^{ti} wynter of age and more, sworn, examyned and diligently required vppon alle the matiers and articlis mynystrid bi the parties aboue reherced, he saith in vertu of his sacrament that he can no thing depose, savyng he saith that on Friday next afore Palme Sonday was twelmonth he wente to the market to bie fisshe, and in his comyng hamward bi Richard Taillouris durre he sawe Roger Champernon standyng in the porche and Nicholas Radeford comyng oute of the durre, and toke his leve of the saide Roger and wente toward the chirche yerde of Seynt Petir. Examyned wher he was whan they departid, he saith that he stode atte Richard Taillouris stalle with a sporiour whiche had receyved money of the saide Champernon for sporis. Examyned what tyme of the day hit was, he saith that the saide Friday betwixt viij and ix afore none. Otherwise he cannought say then he hath saide afore and deposid. He is nought corrupte, as he saith.

John Wykeham, hostiler of the parissh of Seynt Paule of Exceter, xliiij wynter of age and more, sworne, examyned and diligently required vppon alle the articlis reherced in the bill mynystrid bi the parties, he cannought say, save onely he saith that on Monday next after Mighelmasse day last passid the mayer of Exceter was chosyn and the morne vppon, that is to say the Tywesday, as he supposith he sawe a company come oute of Waterbear Strete goyng towarde the High Strete of Exceter. And he axede of folk that wente by the strete 'Who goth ther?', and they said Nicholas Radeford. Axid whether he sawe Nicholas Radeford him selfe in the visage, and he saith nay, but he trowith that hit was Radeford, because the peple saide hit shulde be he. Ferther ne more cannought he depose in the matier contened in the bill. He is nought corrupte, as he saith.

William Undy, glasier of the parissh of Seynt Martyn, xl wynter of age and more, sworne, examyned and diligently required vppon alle the matiers and articlis contenyd in the bill mynystrid by the parties, saith that he can no thing depose, save onely he saith that he sawe Nicholas Radeford atte Exceter on a Friday in Lente whan my lorde of Glouceter was atte Exceter, what Friday hit was in certeyn, he wote nought. As toching othir thing contened in the bill, he cannought depose, save onely as he hath herd of rumour of peple. He is nought corrupte, as he saith.

John Legh, skynner of the parissh of Alle Halowe in the Goldesmyth rew of Exceter, xxx^ti wynter of age and more, sworne, examyned and diligently required of alle the matiers and articlis contened in the bill mynystred bi the parties, saith that he can no thing depose in the matier, save onely he saith that one Benet Skynner of Exceter come to his house and praid him that he wold aspie whether William Tremayn shulde haue eny lyvelode of his fader, and the saide John Legh on a tyme whan he rode to Tavistok inquired amonge peple of the contre ther of his lyvelode, and ther couth no man telle him ther that he had eny lyvelode. And whanne he come home, he tolde the same Benet Skynner as he had herde. And sone after hit happenyd the saide Benet Skynner is wife for to debate with hire owen doughter whiche was maried to the saide William Tremayn, and callid hir harlot and brothell. And she answered hir moder, and saide that she was no brothell, for she was also good as she, and that she had for to shewe for hir in that house. And so the saide Benet Skynner on a tyme wente to his doughter presse and ther he fonde in hir presse a dede, supposyng to saide Benet that hit had bene money whiche he had receyued for his lyvelode, as he saide to this man sworne. And this same dede he broughte and shewid to him the morne after Palme Sonday was twelmonth, as he supposith, sayng in this wise: 'Lo, John Legh, thow toldist me that William Tremayn had no lyvelode, now knowe I the contrarie, for I haue a dede that saith that William Tremayn is lord of Hewissh, for I haue bene with a clerk whiche hath rad hit to me.' Other wise ne more can he nough depose in the matiers contened in the bill than he hath saide afore. He is nought corrupte, as he saith.

William Coppe, panbeter of the parissh of Seynt Poule of Exceter, the age of xl yeer, sworne, examyned and diligently required vppon alle the matiers contened in the bill mynystred bi the parties, he saith that he canne no thing depose, save onely that on Monday next after Mighelmasse day last passid the mayer of Exceter was chosyn and that same Monday he saith that he sawe Nicholas Radeford betwixt x and xj of the belle afore none in the High Strete of Exceter goyng toward the Est yeate, and after none bothe evyn atte nyght in the Northgate Strete goyng to his place in the same strete, and he saith that he lay ther al nyght, and he saith that the saide Nicholas shulde nought haue passid oute of the toune that nyght, but he shulde haue knowen of his goyng, for he duellith next to that place. Examyned how he remembrith him of that Monday rather then of eny other day, he saith as hit is knowen to alle Exceter that ther shal be a certeyn horne blawen afore the eleccion of the mayer, and wher he was atte his werke atte the mayers house that now is to amende a fourneys, he wente fro his werke bitwene vij and viij afore none the saide Monday, as he was prayed bi a wedowe whiche aught blowe that horne that he shulde go aboute the cite in hir stede with him that blewe that horne. Therby he knowith verrely that hit was the same Monday. More of the matier can he nought say ne depose. He is nought corrupte, as he saitht.

Richard Nahilyn, wever of the parissh of Seynt Stephyns of Exceter, l wynter of age and more, sworne, examyned and diligently required vppon alle the matiers contened in the bill mynystred bi the parties, he saith he cannought depose, saue onely he saith that on Monday next after Mighelmasse day last was the mayer of Exceter was chosen, and the morn next vppon, that is to say the Tywesday or els the Wandisday, he cannought redely depose, the after none, what certeyn houre he can noght saye, Nicholas Radeford rode on a white horse afore his durre in the Highstrete of Exceter toward the Est yeate with two men, one afore him and another behinde him, and a man goyng on fute bi his side and <and his hoode ou*er* his schulder>, this he deposith of his sight and knawelege. Other wise can he nought say in the matiers. He is nought corrupte, as he saith.

John Pyper, skynner of the parissh of Seynt Laurence of Exceter, the age of lx wynter and more, sworn, examyned and diligentely required vppon all the matiers and articlis contenid in the bill mynistrid bi the parties, saith that he cannoght depose in the said matier, save onely he saith that William Tremayn come to him aboute this tyme twelmonth, what day in certeyn he cannought depose, and prayd him that he myght haue his horse to hire for a yonge man that shulde ride a certeyn erande of his, and he axid of him what he shulde carie, and he saide no thing, save onely a man and a litel box, and so he lete him haue his horse for that tyme for iij days, and after iij dayes he brought his horse home whan he had done his iourney, and for as moche as his hors was evil done to, he axid 'How haue ye rulid myne horse, William, and what hath myne horse borne?' 'For sothe', he saide, 'no thing save a man and a box with a dede ther in.' And sone after the saide William Tremayn come and hired the saide horse for him selfe, and this man sworne axid him whither he wolde ride, and he saide to on Champernon, to fecche a certeyn su*m*me of gold. And whanne he come home ayen, he wolde pay him for his horse for the bothe iourneys, and he saide that the said Champernon shulde bere him a certeyn of rente yerly. And this man sworne saith ferthermore that the Monday next after Mighelmasse day last passid the mayer of Exceter was chosyn, and the Tywesday or Wandisday next folowyng, whether day in certeyn he wote never, and whether hit wer afore none or after of the two dayes he can nought say, he saith he saw Nicholas Radeford ridyng afore his house oute atte Este yeate and spake to him, wheter hit were a white horse or a gray he cannought depose, and two men ridyng with him and he sawe also a man goyng and talkyng with him bare

[m. 5]

hedid, what man hit was, he wote never. Otherwise no more can he nought depose in the matiers and articlis contenid in the bill. He is nought corrupte, as he saith.

John Wilscomb, cariour of sakkis of the parissh of Seynt Dauid with oute North yeate of Exceter, sworne, examyned and diligently required vppon alle the matiers and articlis contened in the bill mynystrid bi the parties aboue reherced, saith that he can no thing depose, save onely that he saith that on Monday next after Mighelmasse day last passid the mayer of Exceter was chosen and that same Monday he saith that he sawe Nicholas Radeford on Seynt Dauid is doune, ridyng toward Exceter afore none, and ther he watered his horse, and Nicholas Radeforde axed of him and his felaweship what hit was of the clok, and this man sworne saide to him that hit was betwixt viij and ix of the belle. Axed forthermore what men rode with him, he saith that his clerk and his horsman and other mo that he knewe nought. Examyned what causith him to remember of this day more then of a nother and of Radeforde more then of a nother man, he saith that he wente into Exceter with his felowe to ete a pie with other felaweship, and when they were come thider that felaweship had dyned and was gone. And as they turnede ayein vnto the milne, they mette Radeforde ridyng in to the tounewarde, and this man sworne axid of his felawe 'Lorde, what makith Radeford here this day?' 'Trewely', quoth his felowe, 'I trowe that he be come to trete that Upton may be made mayer.' Otherwise can he nought say. He is nought corrupt, as he saith.

John Noreys, skynner of Exceter, the age of xxiiij^{ti} wynter, sworne, examyned and diligently required vppon alle the matiers contened in the bill mynystrid bi the parties, saith that the maier of Exceter was chosen the Monday next after Mighelmasse day last passid and the morne vppon, that is to say the Tywesday, William Tremayn come to this man sworne in Northgate strete betwixt v and vj in the morne tyde and axid of this man where that Radefordis house was, and he saide 'Here aboue', and wente with him to the dore, and the saide Tremayn knokkid atte the wyket and one of Radefordis men come and axid of him what he wolde. He saide that he wolde speke with his maister, and he answerd and saide that he was in his bedde. Examyned, if he sawe Radeford that day, he saith nay. Examyned ferthermor vppon alle the matiers and articles contenid in the bill, he saith he can no thing depose otherwise then he hath saide before. He is nought corrupte, as he saith.

Nicholas Clerk, wever, of the parissh of Seynt Paule, the age of xxvi^{ti} wynter, sworne, examyned a[n]d³ diligently required vppon alle the matiers and articlis contenid in the bill mynystred by the parties, he saith that he can no thing depose, savyng that he saith that on Tywesday sevenynght after Mighelmasse day that last was he mette with Nicholas Radeford and William Tremayn in Waterbere Strete goyng toward North gate strete, and a cloke on his hede, after none, what houre he wote neu*er*. Examyned how he remembreth that hit shulde be that day, he saith be cause that he that day bare ale to Benet Skynneris house. More can he nought depose in the saide matier. He is nought corrupte, as he saith.

Nicholas Coldewille, dwellyng with John Holand, squyer, xxiiij^{ti} wynter of age, sworne, examyned and diligently required vppon alle the matiers and articlis contenid in the billis mynystred bi the parties, he saith he cannought depose in the saide matiers, save onely he saith in a tyme betwixt Ester was twelmonth and Midsomer, what day ne weke he remembrith him nought, William Tremayn sente him to Bier Ferrerz to Roger Champernon with a box closid in lynnyn clothe. And when he come to the saide Champernon is presence, Champernon drewe oute of the lynnyn clothe a box and oute of the box a dede. And whan he had radde the dede, he come to this man sworne and axid of him 'Knowist thow this seale? Is this the olde Nicholas Tremayne is seale?' 'For sothe, Sir', saide he, 'I wote never.' Then said Champernon to this man sworne that William Tremayn shulde sende him a relece vppon that dede,⁴ <and> 'Saye thow to William Tremayn that he drede him of no language, for if he wil be rulid, he shal fare better than he is warre of, and if he will nought, he shall fare the wars.' Of all other thingis declarid to him in generall and speciall, he saith he can none other wise depose then he hath saide afore. Examyned ferthermore with wat wex the dede was sealid, he saith with rede wex. Examyned whether hit semed olde sealid or newe, he saith hit semed him nough righ newe sealid. He is nought corupte, as he saith.

3.   MS 'ad'.
4.   'vn to him' crossed out.

Richard Wode, toker, of the parissh of Seynt Sidewill, xxiiij wynter of age, brought furth by Thomas Tremayn nought wityng that he shulde be examyned, and for as moche as ther is made mencion in the commission that the commissaries shulde inquere vijs et modis[5] etc., they, supposyng that the said Richard shulde haue knowelege of the matiers contenyd in the bill mynystred by Thomas Tremayn aboue saide, made him swere vppon a buke, examynyd him and diligently required him vppon alle the matiers contened in the bill, and in especiell whether he wer maneshed by Radeforde or eny other man for him, he saith by the vertu of his sacrament nay. He saith ferther that a litil afore Lammasse last passid William Tremayn gaf this man sworn a russet hude with a blak tippet for the takyng of a mece of fissh, and Radeford, havyng knowelege that this William Tremayn had geven this man an hode, [sente to him][6] the said hude, supposyng that the hude had ben yeven to this man sworn to corrupe him to depose otherwise then the treuthe in the said matier, he examyned ther vppon saith nay in vertue of his oth. Examynid ferthermore if he were procured by eny of the parties to say eny other then the treuthe in the matier, he saith that William Tremayn spake to him that he shulde haue come afore the commissaries to depose lik as he shulde be infourmyd. Askid if he couthe eny thing in the matier depose of treuth and of his owen knawelege, he saith nay. And he saide to William Tremayn that he wold for no thing offende his conscience. He is nought corrupte, as he saith.

Et Ego, Johannes Polyng clericus, Exoniensis diocesis publicus auctoritate apostolica notarius, premissis omnibus et singulis dum sic, vt premittitur, agerentur et fierent sub annis domini, indiccione, pontificatu, mensibus diebus et locis predictis, regni vero Regis Anglie Henrici sexti post conquestum septimodecimo, presens personaliter interfui eaque omnia et singula sic fieri vidi et audiui, alijsque arduis occupatus negocijs per alium fidelem scribi feci, publicaui et de mandato dictorum venerabilium virorum in dicte inquisicionis et examinacionis negocio commissariorum necnon et ad rogatum dictarum parcium in hanc publicam formam

5. Underlined in MS.
6. MS faded.

redegi, signoq*ue* et no*min*e meis solit*is* et consuet*is* signaui rogatus
et requisitus in fidem et testimonium omnium p*r*emissor*um*.

[*And I, John Polyng, clerk, notary public by apostolic authority
of the diocese of Exeter, personally present have taken part in
the premises, all and singular, when they were, as aforesaid,
enacted and done under the aforesaid years of the lord, indiction,
pontificate, months, days and places, and in the seventeenth year
of the reign of Henry VI, king of England, after the conquest, and
have seen and heard them all and singular so done, and, occupied
with other important affairs, have caused them to be written by
another trustworthy man, have published them, and by the order
of the said venerable men, commissaries in the business of the
said inquisition and examination, and also by the request of the
said parties, have put them in this public form, and signed them
with my habitual and accustomed mark and name, asked and
required for the credence and witness of all the premises.*]

[Notarial mark of Polyng]

[rot. 2,
m. 1]

Robert Willeford, gentilman, the age of xxvj wynter and more,
sworne, examyned and diligently required vppon alle the matiers
contened in the billis mynystred by Thomas Tremayn in that
one party and Nicholas Radeford and Roger Champernon on
that other partie, to him fro worde to word openly redde and
declared, saith thus that wher hit is supposed and reherced in the
saide bill that Roger Champernon, John Colmestorre, John Fitz,
Janyn his horseman, John Bukkeby, and on Totewill his men and
William Tremayn shuld soupe atte Radefordes place in Cory Lane
the Thursday next after that my lorde of Glouceter was passid
estward from Exceter, was nought sothe, for he saith that the
Friday and Saterday after the departyng of Radeford to the assise
of Launceston the first weke in Lente Thomasie the wife of the
saide Radeford remeuede oute of Cory Lane in Exeter fro the
place wher that her husbonde duellid in before into Northgate
Strete with alle hir*e* household into William Upton is house, and
ther her*e* husbond and sheo contynewid her*e* houshold til they

remeved to his owen place <callid> Uppecote by his consciens. Also he saith that he was with the saide Thomasyn the Friday next after that she was remeued fro Corylane in to Northgate Strete to Upton is place, and ther he was with hir the Monday, Tywesday, Wandisday and Thursday and dranke with hir euere day of thes dayes afore saide. Item the xiiij day of Aprill, ther as he that is sworne hath saide aboue that the saide Thomasie remeued on Friday, he better remembrid saith that she began to remove the Saterday and was fully remeved the Monday nex sewyng, and that he deposith of his verrey sciens. Item wher hit is made mencion in the said bill that on Thursday next vppon a shire, as hit is contened in the article, at Shillyngford is hous at Exceter were present Nicholas Radeford, William Tremayn, John Shillyngford and other, as hit is contened in the said article, the forsaid Robert Willeford aboue sworne saith and deposith that vppon a Thursday next after a shire (what shire in certeyn he remembrith him nought, wel he wote hit was betwixt Mighelmasse and Cristis masse) he was present in the saide Shillyngfordis hous atte Exceter with the mayer and foure other of his officers, that is to saye Vincent Hert and thre sargeantis, beyng ther present Nicholas Radeford, William Tremayn, John Shillyngford, Gylot Baker, John Kyrton, John Wolston and other, wher that he herde the saide William Tremayn examyned by Nicholas Radeford vppon the makyng of a fals dede by the whiche the saide Nicholas Radeford was diffamed, knowelegid oponly afore the persones afore saide that the copie of the same dede was made by on Bithelake and nought by Nicholas Radeford and delivered to the saide William Tremayn by the saide Bithelake at the Blake auter in Seynt Petris chirche. Item the said Robert seith wher as the forsaide William Tremayn saith that the forsaide Nicholas shulde offre the forsaid William an hundreth nobles for to say that the dede aforsaide was i made and forgeid by the saide Bithelake, or for to go oute of the countre, he saith and deposith that also longe as he was ther present he sawe none suche offeryng ne proffer of the saide Nicholas to the forsaide William in no wise i do. Other wise ne in none other maner he can nought depose of the matier contened in the bill than he hath aforsaide. He is nought corrupte by preyer ne price, as he saith by his sacrament.

Sir Robert Nywenham, prest and person of the parissh chirche of Poughill, the age of lii wynter and more, sworn, examyned and diligently required vppon all the matiers contened in the bill aboue nevened, he saith by the vertu of his sacrament made with his right honde vppon the crosse and <u>Te igit*ur*</u> and deposith ther as hit is saide that Nicholas Radeford shuld haue bene atte Exceter on Monday next after Mighelmasse day last passid, that the forsaid Nicholas was oute of Exceter atte a place of his owen called Uppecote viij myle oute of Exceter the Sonday, Monday <next after the saide Mighelmasday>, Tywesday, Wandisday and Thursday than next after folowyng, excepte that the Tywesday he rode to my lorde of Deuenshire atte a place callid Tydecomb and come home ayein to his mete the fornone. And the Friday next folowyng he toke his iourney toward London and this same man that is sworne rode with him in the way til he come to a place called Bradeway in Som*erset*. Examyned how he knowith that Radeford was oute of Exceter and atte his owen hous and place afor saide the Sonday, Monday, Tywesday, Wandisday and Thursday, he saith of his certeyn sciens and of his sight, for he was all this tyme with him *p*resent vp risyng and doune liggyng in his owen house and place aforsaide. Item axed and examyned if he can eny other thing depose vppon alle the other matiers contened in the bill whiche he hath[7] redde fro worde to worde, he saith that he can none other wise depose than he hath saide afore. He is nought corrupte by price ne preyer, as he saith.

Robe*r*t Legh, frankeleyn and citeseyn of Exceter, the age of lx wynter and more, sworne, examyned and diligently required vppon all the matiers contened in the bill abowe nevened, saith that wher hit is conteyned in the said bill that on Monday next after Mighelmasse day last passed Nicholas Radeford shulde haue bene at Exceter in Northgate Strete etc. he saith that hit is vntrewe, and that he knowith in so moche as he had the keyes of the place whiche Nicholas Radeford dwellid in Cory Lane in his kepyng that tyme, and also he duellith now and did atte that tyme in North gate strete right auentis the place whiche Nicholas Radeford holdith of William Uppeton, and alle that Monday he sawe nought the said Nicholas, ne the Tywesday next after, and if he had bene atte Exceter, he saith that he shulde haue had knowelege ther of. Item examyned ferther vppon the partie of the

7.   MS 'hath hath'.

bill wher that hit is said that the Thursday next after that my
lorde of Glouceter was passede estward oute of Exceter, Roger
Champernon, Nicholas Radeford and other mo shulde haue
souped in Corylane atte Nicholas Radefordis house etc., he saith
that hit is nought sothe in so moche, that he saith of his verrey
sciens that Nicholas Radeford is houshold was fully remeued fro
Cory Lane into Northgate Strete the first weke of clene Lente next
afore the saide Thursday contened in the bill. And ferthermore he
saith that the saide Thursday and Friday next afore Palme Sonday
was twelmonth the said Nicholas Radeford was nought in the
place in Corylane, for he supposith that he was atte his place calle
Uppecote viij myle fro Exceter. Item examyned whether he sawe
the saide Nicholas at Exceter in eyther of the saide two dayes, he
saith that he remembrith him that he sawe him nought the two
dayes in no place. Otherwise he cannought depose of the matiers
contened in the said bill. He is nought corrupte by preyer ne price,
as he saith.

Sir William Hamond, prest, porcionary of the first porcion
in the parisshe chirche of Tyuerton, xxxvj wynter of age and
more, sworne, examyned and diligently required what he can
say vppon the matier contened in the bill aboue neuend, he saith
that the secunde weke of clene Lente was a twelmonth this man
that is sworne was sente fro my lorde of Deuonshire to Nicholas
Radeford to fecche with him a boke of cronycles, and when he
come to Exceter the saide Nicholas was gone to the assise atte
Launceston, and then he wente and soughte his wife and fonde
hire in a place in Northgatestrete that is callid Uptons place, and
askid the saide boke of cronycles of hir, and she saide that hit was
with a writer in the toune, and so he saith of his knowelege that
Nicholas Radeford was remeued fro the place in Cory lane in to
Northgate Strete, and ther he duellid atte that tyme. Examyned
forthermore if he can eny othir thing say in the saide matier, he
saith that Roger Champernon, of the whiche the said bill makith
mencion, was with my lorde of Deuenshire on Monday next before
Palme Sonday was a twelmonth atte Colmp John, the Tywesday
ridyng toward Colcomb, the Wandisday, Thursday and Friday
next after til hit was passid mydday the said Champernon was
with my lorde of Deuenshire atte Colcomb, and this he saith of
his verrey sciens. Item he saith that on Tywesday seuenygh after
Mighelmasday next passed the said Sir William Hamond saith

that he mette with the said Nicholas Radeford to Tidecomb ward
toward my lorde of Deuenshire. And the said Nicholas saide whan
he partid for my said lord, that he wolde go home. Item examyned
wher the saide Nicholas was the Monday next afore, he saith as
he had informacion of John Dirwill that he was that day atte his
owen place called Uppecote. Item he saith tha[t][8] on Thursday next
sewyng the said Sir William was with Radeforde atte his place
called Uppecote and fette with him a presentacion for the chirch
of Crewis Morchard. Otherwise ne more can nought he depose of
the matier contened in the bill, as he saith. He is nought corrupte
by preyer ne price, as he saith.

   Thomas Wellywrought, stiward of my lord of Devonshires
housholde, the age of xl wynter and more, sworne, examyned and
diligently required vppon al the matiers and articles conteyned
in the bill aboue nevened, saith that vppon Monday next afore
Palme Sonday was twelmonth Roger Champernon was with my
lorde of Deuonshire atte Colump John, and that day my forsaide
lord remeued toward his maner of Colcomb and lay that nyght at
Jankyn Laurence is house besidis Seynt Mary Otery, and the saide
Roger in his company, and dyned ther the morne, that is to say
the Tywesday next folowyng, and fro that straught to Colcomb,
and the saide Roger with him, and was ther contynewelly abidyng
Wandisday, Thursday and Fryday next folowyng til they had eten,
and this he saith of his certeyn sight and sciens, and also bi the
briefs of his lordis housholde. As toching the Monday next after
Mighelmas day last passed he can nought depose, ne of none other
matiers contened in the said bill, otherwise then he hath deposed.
He is nought corrupte by price ne prayer, as he saith.

[m. 2]

Sir John Hoigge, preste, parson of Rawisaysshe, xxxv wynter of
age and more, sworne, examyned and diligently required of all
the matiers and articlis contened in the bill aboue nevened, saith
that the Monday nex after Mighelmasse day last passed he was
atte Poughill, wher that he spake with John Wolstone, whiche was
comen thider forto holde courte, and ther he axede of the said

---

8. MS 'than'.

Wolstone whether that Nicholas Radeford were atte home atte
Uppecote, and he saide yee, and forthermore the saide Wolston
saide to this man sworne that Radeford wold ride on the morne
after to my lorde of Deuenshire, beyng that tyme atte Tydecomb.
Item axed whether he sawe Radeford the saide Monday, he saith
nay, but he saith that he sawe him the Sonday atte nyght afore
atte Poughill, and dranke ther of the chirche ale, and sawe a man
of Maister John Waryns speke with him ther. Otherwise ne more
can he nought depose of all the matiers conteyned in the bill. He is
nought corrupte by price ne preyer, as he saith.

   John Dyrwill of Tyu*er*ton, cordewayner, xl^{ti} wynter of age and
more, sworne, examyned and diligently required vppon alle the
matiers and articles contened in the bill aboue nevened, and in
especiel of the *pre*sence and absence of Nicholas Radeforde the
Monday nex after Mighelmasse day next passid, he saith that by
co*m*maundement of my lord of Devonshire he come to Nicholas
Radefordis place atte Uppecote the saide Monday bitwixt vj and
vij of the belle in the mornyng, and ther he fonde and sawe the
saide Nicholas come doune of his chamber, his hose aboute his
kneys and vngerd, and bade him bryng his houndes and come to
my lorde of Deuenshire, and he excused him and saide that he
wold be with him the morne and gafe him a grote for his message,
and the [morne]^9 folowyng the saide Radeford come bityme aboute
vij of the belle to Tyu*er*ton and callid this man that is sworne
by his name and bade him go with him to Tydecomb to my lord
of Deuenshire, and so he did and left him ther with my lorde of
Deuenshe, and so wente home ayen to Tyuerton to his owen house.
As toching all other thinges conteyned in the bill of articlis and
matiers aboue reherced, he can none otherwise depose then he
hath saide before. He is nought corrupte by price ne prayer, as he
saith.

   William Bisshop, vnderstiward of my lorde of Deuonshires
londes, xl wynter of age and more, sworne, examyned and
diligently required vppon alle the matiers and articles conteyned
in the bill aboue nevened, saith that on Thursday next afore Palme
Sonday was twe[l]month^{10} he come to Colcomb and helde courte

9.   MS 'more'.
10. MS 'twemonth'.

atte Coleton afore none, and come atte even to Colcomb and ther
he fonde Roger Champernon, and the Friday next after the said
William and Roger dyned togider at Colcomb, and atte thre after
none they come rydyng togeder to Exceter ward, and bitwixt vij
and viij atte nyght they come to Exceter and alight atte Richard
Orengis house, and ther they drank togeder and departed for that
nyght. Otherwyse ne more can he nought depose of all the matier
and articles conteyned in the said bill. He is nought corrupte by
prayer ne price, as he saith.

John Person, skynner, dwellyng with Walter Mirefeld, skynner
of Exceter, of the parissh of Seynt Petrokis, the age of xxv^{ti} wynter,
sworn, examyned and diligently required vppon the matier and
articles conteyned in the bill aboue saide, he saith by the vertu of
his sacrament that the mayer of Exceter was chosyn the Monday
next after Mighelmasday last passid, and the morne ther vppon
this man now sworne saith that he drad him to be arreste to the
pees atte the sute of one Alison Fynkham, wherfore he rode toward
Nicholas Radefordis place called Uppecote, and whan he come a
myle fro Uppecote, he mette with one John Somerhay atte a place
called Raddon Fourcheis and axid of him, if Radeford were atte
his place of Uppecote, and he saide nay, for he was riden to my
lorde of Deuenshire, and so this man sworne turnede home ayein
to Exceter, and also sone as he was came with in North gate of
Exceter, he was arreste to the pees by one John Bowedon, that
tyme sergeant, atte the sute of the saide Alison Fynkham, and
i ladde to the yelde halle, and sone after fonde borwes and was
delyuered oute of pryson. Inquired and axede whether he can eny
otherwise depose in the matiers conteyned in the bill, and he saith
nay, saue onely as he hath deposid before. Item inquired by the
vertu of his sacrament whether he hath receyved eny money to
depose in this matier, or eny is to him promysed, and he saith nay,
saue onely that William Tremayn cam to him in the cathedrall
chirche of Seynt Petri of Exceter and axed of this man now
sworne, if he couthe depose eny thyng of the Thursday nex afore
Palme Sonday was twelmonth, or the Friday next folowyng, and
of the Tywesday next after the mayer was chosen aboue reherced,
and the saide John Person answerd and saide to the saide William
Tremayn that he couth no thyng depose of the saide Thursday and
Friday. And then the saide William Tremayn promysede to this
same man i sworne xl d., if he wold depose in examynacion that

he had sene Nicholas Radeford atte Exceter the saide Thursday and Friday next afore Palmesonday was twelmonth, and he saide that he wold nought so depose for no good, for hit was vntreuth after his consciens and kneweliche, and saide to him that ferther then he knewe he wolde nought depose, and so the saide William in grete wrath departid fro him and saide that he wold quite him in the warst wise. Otherwise can he nought depose of the matier and articlis contened in the bill. He is nought corrupte by preyer ne price, as he saith.

John Bisshop, ferro*ur*, duellyng with my lord Botreaux, xlvj wynter of age and more, sworn, examyned and diligently required of all the matiers contened in the bill, he saith by the vertu of his sacrament that he can no thing depose, saue onely ther as hit is supposid and writon in the saide bill that Nicholas Radeford shuld haue bene atte Exceter the Monday next after Mighelmas day that last was, he saith that he come to Uppecote the Sonday atte even next after the saide Mighelmasse day, and ther he abode alle that nyght, and the saide Monday all day, and the Tywesday til after none. Inquired whether the saide Nicholas Radeford wer ther alle that tyme, and he saith that the saide Nicholas that Sonday atte nyght and Monday al day he was atte home, and the Tywesday in the mornyng he rode to my lorde of Deuenshire to Tydecomb and come home to Uppecote to his mete, and this he deposith of his verrey sight and knowelege, for he was atte Uppecote al that tyme. Of al other articles expouned to him in gen*er*all, he saith he can no thing depose otherwise then he hath saide afore. He is nought corrupte, as he saith.

Henry Mabbe, yeman of my lorde of Deuenshires, xxx*ti* wynter of age and more, sworne, examyned and diligently required vppon all the matier*s* reherced in the bill, saith that he can no thing depose, neyther of the absence ne p*re*sence, saue onely as he hath herd of his felawes. He is nought corrupte, as he saith.

Maister John Maior, person of Crewis Morchard, duellyng in houshold with my lord of Deuenshire, the age of xl*ti* wyntr, sworne, examyned and diligently required vppon the articlis conteyned in the bill, and in especiel whether Roger Champernon wer with my lord of Deuenshire atte Colcomb the Thursday and Fryday afore Palme Sonday was twelmonth other no, he saith he can no thing depose of his verrey sciens, save onely as he hath herd of diverse p*er*sones of the housholde credible to his consciens. Axed of whome, he saith of S*ir* William Hamond, p*ar*son of Tyu*er*ton, Thomas Wellewrought, stiward of the houshold, and other credible p*er*sones of the saide houshold, that the saide Roger Champ*er*non was atte Colcomb on Thursday and Friday til he had dyned. Also required if he can eny more say in the said matier, he saith nay. He is nought corrupte, as he saith.

Nicholas Tremayll, squyer of my lord of Deuenshire, the age of xx^{ti} wynter, sworn, examyned and diligently required of alle the matiers reherced in the bill, saith that Roger Champernon was atte Colcomb the Thursday and Friday til after none next afore Palme Sonday was twelmonth, and was in purpose to haue go thens the saide Thursday, save that my lorde made him abide stil ther til on Friday after none for the comyng of a knyght callede Sir Stephen Popham of Hampton shire. Otherwise ne more can he nought depose of the matiers contened in the bill. He is nought corrupte, as he saith.

John Prewe, my lorde of Deuenshire is barbo*ur*, the age of xxij^{ti} wynter, sworne, examyned and diligently required vppon alle the matiers reherced in the bill, acordith in his deposicion worde by worde with Nicholas Tremayll nex aboue examyned. He is nought corrupte, as he saith.

Richard Nele, boteler with my lord of Deuenshire, xxiij wynter of age, sworne, examyned and diligently required of alle the matiers contened in the bill, acordith in all his deposicion with the saide Nicholas Tremayll aboue examyned. He is nought corrupte, as he saith.

Walter Owyntyn, vssher of my lorde of Deuenshires halle, xxx^{ti} wynter of age, sworne, examyned and diligently required vppon all the matier conteyned in the bill, acordith worde by worde with Nicholas Tremayll aboue examyned. He is nought corrupte, as he saith.

John Pye, warderober with my lorde of Deuenshire, xxx^{ti} wynter of age, sworne, examyned and diligently required of all the matier specified in the bill, acordith worde by worde in all his deposicion with Nicholas Tremayll aboue examyned. He is nought corrupte, as he saith.

Aleyn Holme, panter with my lorde of Deuenshire, xxiiij^{ti} wynter of age and more, sworne, examyned and diligently required vppon alle the circumstance contened in the bill, saith that he can no thing depose, savyng he saith that Roger Champernon was with

my lorde of Deuenshire atte Colcomb Tywesday, Wandisday and
Thursday next afore Palme Sonday was twelmonth. Inquired of
the Friday, he saith he was ther til he had dyned. Examyned how
he knowith this, he saith as he hath herd of his felawship, and
suppose hit trewe in his conscience. None other

[m. 3]

thing ne other wise can he nought depose as touching the matier
contened in the bill. He is nought corrupte by preyer ne price, as
he saith.

John Fitz, gentilman of the parissh of Tavistok, the age of xxviij
wynter and more, sworne, examyned and diligently required of all
the matiers contened in the grete bill mynystred by Thomas Tremayn
to him worde by worde radde fro the begynnyng to the ende, he
saith by the vertu of his sacrament that he can no thing depose in
the saide matier, saue onely that he saith that he remembrith him
that William Tremayn was with Roger Champernon atte the mete
atte Richard Taillours hous of Exceter in assise tyme, what assise
and yeer he can nought depose. Item examyned if he can depose
of the makyng of eny fals dedis, of the whiche is made mencion in
the said bill, he saith nay. Examyned if he haue seyne eny dede of
feoffement the whiche Nicholas Tremayn shulde make to William
Tremayn, his son, of the maner of North Hewyssh, he saith that
he sawe a dede shewid to him by his maister Roger Champernon
sithen Mighelmasse last passed, whiche dede, as he saith, made
mencion that Nicholas Tremayn shulde yeue and graunte in fee to
William Tremayn, his sonne, the maner of North Hewissh with
avoweson of the churche to haue and to hold in fee. Examyned
ferthermore what he suppose of the dede, whether hit be trewe
other fals, he saith he wote neuer, wel he wote hit is a fair dede to
the sight. Examyned wherwith the dede was sealid, he saith hit was
sealid with reed wex with a seale contenyng a skalap. Otherwise
ne in none other maner he can nought depose, then he hath saide
afore. He is nought corrupte, as he saith.

Sir William Cheke, chapeleyn with Roger Champernon, squyer,
xxx^ti wynter of age and more, sworne, examyned and diligently
required vppon all the articlis and matier contened in the bill, he
saith in vertu of his sacrament that he can no thing say ne depose
ther in. Examyned in especiell vppon an article makyng mencion

that vppon Friday next afore Seynt Mighell day last passid William
Tremayn was atte Bear Ferrerz, and that day Roger Champernon
come fro Launceston and saide that Radeford and he were acordid
atte Launceston that he shulde sende the date of the saide forgid
dede with the wittenesse, and then the saide Champernon fette
the dede and bade the saide Sir William Cheke his preste to write
the date of that dede and the names of the wittenesse in a scrowe.
Uppon this article this man sworne, diligently examyned, saith in
vertu of his sacrament that this article is vntrewe in him self, for
he saith bi his prestehode that he was neuer previe to this matier,
ne his maister Roger Champernon ne none other for him bade him
write the date of the dede nor the names of the wittenesse, as hit is
surmyttid in the article. Axid ferthermore if he can eny other thing
depose in the saide matier, he saith nay, savyng onely that he hath
herd by the comon rumo*ur* of the peple that William Tremayn
shuld bryng Roger Champernon in possession of the maner of
North Hewissh, divers tymes he has seyn William Tremayn with
his said maister atte Bier Ferrerz, what he did ther or what his
erand was, he can nought say. More ne other wise than thus as
he hath deposid cannought he say in the matier. He is nought
corrupte, as he saith.

John Colmestorr*e*, gentilman of the parissh of Tavistok, lx^{ti}
wynter of age and more, sworn, examyned and diligently required
vppon all the grete bill mynystred by Thomas Tremayn redde to
him worde by worde fro the begynnyg vnto the ende, he saith in
vertu of his sacrament that he knowith of his verrey sciens no
worde, ne was never p*r*esent ne pryue, as hit is surmyttid in the
bill, in no maner of wirching in this matier. Examyned if he haue
sene eny dede fals other trewe after his conceyte in this matier,
he saith nay. He saith that he was Nicholas Tremaynes feid man
xxx^{ti} wynter or more, and for that cause, as he suppose, the saide
Roger wolde nought lete him be pryue in this matier in no wise.
Examyned if he haue herde of this matier, he saith yea, as the
comon rumo*ur* rynneth amonges the puple, and none other wise.
Examyned if he can depose eny thing of the dayes contened in the
bill mynystred by Radeford, whether he was absent other p*r*esente,
he cannought say. He is nought corrupt as he saith.

Sir John Wolston, preste, p*ar*son of Lansant in Cornewale, l
wynter of age and more, sworne, examyned and diligently required
of alle the matier contened in the bill, saith that xiiij dayes and

more afore Thursday next afore Palmesonday was twelmonth
Nicholas Radeford remeued his householde oute of Cory Lane in
to Northgate Strete, and as he suppose neyther ete ne souped in
the said place afterward, for his stuffe was caried fro the said place
in Cory Lane into Northgate Stre[te][11]. Examyned whether he se
Radeford atte Exceter the Thursday next afore Palmesonday afore
saide, he saith that of his knawelege Radeforde soped with a prest
callid Sir Symon Chuddelegh vppon a Thursday, what Thursday
hit was, he remembrith him nought, whether hit was the Thursday
next afore Passion Sonday or Palme Sonday, he wote nought.
Examyned vppon all other articles contened in the bill mynystred
by the parties, he saith he can no thing depose otherwise then he
hath saide afore. He is nought corrupte, as he saith.

Sir John Fouler, prest, the age of xl wynter and more, sworn,
examyned and diligently required vppon alle the articles and
matier contened in the bill abouue nevened, he saith he can no
thing depose, savyng he saith that the weke a fore Passion Sonday
was twelmonth, what day in certeyn he can nought depose, he
come to Nicholas Radeford into Northgate Strete, where he fonde
him and his wife bothe in a place called 'Uptons place' to speke
with him to haue his counsel in certeyn matiers that he had to
done, and he saith that he had sought him afore in Corylane
wher he supposid to haue founden him, and ther was one that
saide to him that he was remeved thens in to North gate strete
and so he wente thider and fonde him ther and his houshold, and
ther he fonde with him atte that tyme John Coteler and Sir John
Wolston. More ne otherwise then thus can he nought depose in
the matier and articlis contened in the bill. He is nought corrupt,
as he saith.

William Uppeton, citeseyn and ypothecarye of Exceter, of the
parissh of Seynt Martyn, the age of l wynter, sworne, examyned
and diligently required of all the matiers contened in the bill aboue
reherced to him openly redde, he saith that he can no thing depose,
saue only that he saith that the first weke of Lente was twelmonth
the assises wer atte Exceter, and the next weke after were the
assises at Launceston, and ther was Radeford, and that same weke
of this man is certeyn sciens and knoweleche Nicholas Radeford

11. MS 'Stre'.

is wife remeued with all hir householde oute of Corylane in to Northgatestrete. Examyned how he knowith this, he saith that ther was no day that Radeford was at Launceston atte the assises, but that Radeford is wife was atte this mannys hous. He saith forthermore that also sone as Radeford was come fro Launceston, that was in the ende of the secunde weke of Lente, he come streght to his hous in Northgate Strete whiche he rentid of this man now sworne and ther helde his household and come nought after in Cory Lane, also fer furth as he knowith, by the othe and sacrament that he hath made. More ne otherwise cannought he depose of the matier reherced in the bill, ne in no thing pertenyng therto. He is nought corrupte, as he saith.

Sir John Boryngton, parson of the parissh chirche of Seynt Mary the more of Exceter, xxx^ti wynter of age and more, sworne, examyned and diligently required of al the matiers contened in the bill abouue nevened, saith that he cannought depose, savyng onely that he saith that on Seynt Gregory is day was twelmonth this man now sworne saith by the vertu of his sacrament that he was atte Nicholas Radefordes house in North gate strete with the saide Nicholas wife, and ther was that same tyme the said Nicholas household. Examyned how that he knowith this, he saith that he was for the more partie of that terme dayly atte the saide Nicholas table. Axed wher the saide Nicholas was that time, he saith atte the assise of Launceston, as he herd saye. Examyned what he can depose of the Thursday next afore Palmesonday was twelmonth, he saith of his certeyn sciens and knowelege that on Wandisday next afore Palmesonday was twelmonth aboute tweyn of the clokke after none he sawe Nicholas Radeford and his wife with other certeyn of his meynye ridyng oute of Exceter toward a place of his callede Uppecote ix myle oute of Exceter, as he supposeth, and was absente oute of Exceter the Thursday next folowyng, and the Friday he come ayein to Exceter aboute vj of the clok after none. Examyned how he can depose of his absence the Thursday, he saith be cause he was atte Radefordis house that Thursday atte mete and souper with his meynye and that causith him to knowe that he was nought ther, and was on Friday atte Nicholas Radefordis house in Northgate strete atte his comyng home. He is nought corrupte, as he saith.

Thomas Thorp, goldesmyth of the parissh of Alle Halowe in the Goldesmythre, xxxiiij^ti wynter of age and more, sworne, examyned and diligentely required vppon alle the matier contened in the bill mynystred bi the parties in generall declared to hym, he saith he can no thing depose, saue onely ther that hit is specified in the saide bill that William Tremayn shulde come to Tilman Goldesmyth, and Radeford is clerk with him, to amende the corners of the scalib in the seal, as hit is contened in the bill, and more ouere ther as hit is saide in the bille that Tilman Goldesmyth excused him of the mendyng of the seale by age and febelnesse of sight, and be cause there of bade him go to Thomas, his felawe, for he was more sherper of sight than he, he saith in trouth and in certeyn sciens of this matier that William Tremayn come to him in a soler, wher that he sat aboue by him selfe alone and no creature with him, and payed him to amende a faute in the saide seal of lede in the whiche was graven a scaleb, of the whiche scaleb fauted a greyn in the corners. Examyned whether he amendid the corners of the scaleb, as hit is surmyttid in the bill, he saith yee. Examyned also if Radefordes clerk come with William Tremayn to him to amende this seale, he saith by the vertu of his sacrament that William Tremayn come all one bi him selfe, and ther was neyther Radefordis clerk ne none other man with him. And ther as hit is seide in the bille that Radeford is clerk shulde say whan that Thomas Goldesmyth askid what they wold do with the seale, to sele a lettre there wyth, [h]e[12] saith hit is fals, for ther was no man saue onely William Tremayn and this man sworne. Axed whether he knewe Radefordis clerk fro an other man, he saide yee, for they were longe tyme be fore conuersant togiders. Examyned ferther of all[13] other matiers in the bill, he saith he can no thing depose, savyng as he hath deposid before. He is nought corrupte by price ne preyer, as he saith.

[m. 4]

John Crosse, sadeler of the parissh of Seynt Kierens, xl wynter of age, sworne, examyned and duely required of al the matiers contened in the bill in generall and in speciall, he saith he can no thing depose, saue onely he saith that on Wandisday next afore Palmesonday was twelmonth at tweyn of the bel after none

12. MS 'se'.
13. MS 'a all'.

Nicholas Radeford and his wife rode oute of Exceter to their place callede Uppecote and come nought ayein til on the Friday next folowyng aboute sex of the bel after none and that he deposith of his verrey sciens, for he was with his doughter and other of his seruantis in his place in Northgatestrete the moost parte of his absence. Examyned if he can depose whether Nicholas Radeford were atte Exceter the Monday next after Mighelmasse day last passede, he saith of his verrey sciens that he was nought ther. Axed how he knowith hit, he saith be cause that he kepeth the keyes of his place alwais whan he goth oute of the toune, and hath this two yeer and more. Examyned if he can eny thyng depose whether Radeford, Champernon and other nevened in the bill were at soper in Corylane the Thursday next afore Palme Sonday was twelmonth, he saith nay of his verrey knowelege and sciens, for he kept the keyes of the place in Cory Lane that Radeford duellid in afore. He saith forthermore whan that Radeford rode oute of the toune of Exceter on Wandisday afore saide, that Radeford delyuered the keyes of the said place in Cory Lane and bade him that if Seyntclere come to toune the mene tyme, he shulde delyuere him the keyes. The saide Seyntclere come nought to Exceter til after Ester, and then he delyuerede him the keyes, and no rather. And al the mene tyme the keyes were in this man is warde that now is sworne, and in none other. He is nought corrupte, as he saith.

William Chidelegh, gentilman, the age of xxx^ti wynter and more, sworne, examyned and diligently required vppon all the articles contened in the bill, he saith he can no thing depose, but onely that the sessions of the pees were the Wandisday nex after Mighelmasday last passid at Kyrton, wher this man sworne with his maister and brother Sir Philip Courtenay, knyght, was that same day afore saide, and fro thens remeued him to a place of his called Cadlegh, and fro that place he sent this gentil man now sworne to Sir William Palton is wife, prayng hire to be atte chirching of his wife on Sonday next folowyng, and so she was; and vppon Monday next folowyng the saide Sir William Palton is wife remeued towardis Kirton[14] in pilgremage and abode ther al nyght. The morne vppon, that is to say the Tywesday, she dined

14. Crediton.

with John Copleston, and fro thens she rode toward her owen place, and in the ridyng she rode by Radefordis place callede Uppecote and drank with Radeford and his wife, bothe beyng atte home, this gentilman al way beyng present, and this he deposith of his sight and of his sciens. Examyned what tyme of the day hit was that the forsaide Ladie drank with Radeford, he saith as he supposith betwixt tweyn and thre, or els at foure after none. He is nought corrupte, as he saith.

Sir James Richard, parson of the parissh chirche of Seynt Olaue in the cite of Exceter, the age of xxx^ti wynter and more, sworne, examyned and diligently required of alle the matiers contened in the bill mynystred by the parties, he saith that he can no thing depose, savyng that he saith ther as hit is surmyttid in the bill mynystrid by Thomas Tremayn that Nicholas Radeford shulde be atte souper in Cory Lane the Thursday next afore Palme Sonday was twelmonth, he saith of his verrey knowelege that Nicholas Radeford and his wife with all her household were remeued oute of Cory Lane into Northgate strete into a place callede Uptons place and ther was afore Passion Sonday residently, he and his meynye. Examyned what causith him to remembre him that he was ther and his household remeued as he hath saide, he saith that he and one of his felawis callid Sir John Fouler sought Radeford atte his place in Cory Lane afore Passion Sonday was a twelmonth, what day he remembrith him nought, and fonde him nought ther, and then they wente in to Northgate strete and ther they fande him and spake with him, and ther was, as he hath aforsaid, him selfe, his wife and alle his householde. Otherwise then he hath saide can he nought depose bi the othe and sacrament that he hath made. He is nought corrupte, as he saith.

Maister John Thryng, notary publik, proctour generall of the consistorie of Exceter, the age of xxx^ti wynter and more, sworne, examyned and diligently required what he can depose in the matiers mynystred bi the parties rehersed in the bill, he saith that he can no thing depose, savyng that he saith that on Monday next after Mighelmasse day last passet this man sworne was atte a place called Cruwis Morchard to inquere the voydance of the churche,[15] and aboute ten of the clok the same day come thider

15. *The Register of Edmund Lacy, Bishop of Exeter, 1420–1455* ed. G.R. Dunstan (5 vols., Torquay, 1963–72), ii. 107.

Wolstone, Radeforde is son in lawe, as counseler to one of the parties presentid to the chirche, and whan they had done, the said Wolston prayed this man sworne to dyne with his fader in lawe at Uppecote. He wente furth with him, and when he come to Uppecote, he fonde Radeford and his wife atte the dyner and other peple with ham, and then this man sworne sate him doune and dyned, and was ther comonyng with the saide Radeforde til hit was thre of the clok after none, and then he toke his leve rydyng towardis Exceter. And as he was comyn iij myle thens, as he supposith, he mette Frere Courteys. The saide Frere axide of him whens he come, and he said: 'Fro Radeford is hous.' And the frere saide: 'I am thiderwardis.' More as tochyng the matiers rehersed in the bill can he nought say. He is nought corrupte, as he saith.

Thomas Mortymer, husbandman of the parissh of Poughill, the age of l^ti wynter, sworne, examyned and diligently required of al the matiers contened in the bill mynystred bi the parties, he saith he can no thing depose, saue onely that he saith ther that hit is surmyttid that Nicholas Radeford, Roger Champernon, William Tremayn and other shuld haue bene atte soper in Cory Lane the Thursday next afore Palme Sonday was twelmonth, he saith that hit is vn trewe, for Nicholas Radeford had remeued his wife and his household oute of Cory Lane into Northgatestrete the secunde weke of clene Lente before the Thursday, as hit is surmyttid. Examyned how he knowith this, he saith that he was atte Exceter with Radeford is wife the Friday in the secunde weke of clene Lent afore saide and wote well of his verrey knowelege and sciens that his houshold was holy in Northgate Strete and fully remeued fro Cory Lane. Examyned what he can say of the Thursday next afore Palme Sonday was twelmonth, he saith in his consciens also farre as he supposith that the said Nicholas was atte Uppecote the Thursday afore saide. And wel he wote of his verrey sciens that he was with him on Thursday, and that same Thursday as he supposith. Examyned what he can say of the Tywesday <sevenyght> next after Mighelmasse day last passid, as hit is rehersed in the articlis, he saith that Nicholas Radeford was atte his place called Uppecote the Sonday and Monday next after Mighelmasse last passed, and the same Monday myne olde ladie of Deuenshire sente a man of hirs callede Knowdeston for Radeford to come to hir, and he excusid him for that day and wente the morne be tyme to my lorde of Deuenshire, hir sonne, and hir to a place called Tydecombe, and come ayeyn to his owen house by xij of the clok atte none and abode atte home alle that day and the Wandisday after of his verrey knoweligge and sciens, for he is the next neghtebour duellyng to him. He is nought corrupt, as he saith.

Sir Thomas Heye, preste, the age of xxvj^{ti} wynter, sworne, examyned and diligently required of all the matiers contened in the bill mynystred bi the parties, he saith of Sonday, Monday <next after Mighelmasday last passid>, Tywesday and Wandisday than next after folowyng, he saith as Thomas Mortymer saith, the wittenesse next aboue examyned, and that he saith and deposith of his verrey knowlege, for he was stille alle that tyme in Radeforde is houshold. Other thing ne more can nought he depose of the matier contened in the saide bill. He is nought corrupt, as he saith.

Frere John Courteys, doctour of diuinite, the age of xxxvj^{ti} wynter and more, saith in verbo sacerdocij that, as tochyng the matier in generall, he can nought depose, savyng he saith that on Sonday nex after Mighelmasse day last passid he saide a sermon in the college chirche of Kirton[16], and the morne vppon, that is to say the Monday next folowyng, he went toward Radefordis house called Uppecote, and was with him ther atte soper and alle nyght, and the Tywesday in the mornyng be tymes he wente home to Exceter. More cannought he depose in the matier. He is nought corrupte, as he saith.

Richard Isaak of Crewis Morchard, carpenter, the age of xl wynter and more, sworne, examyned and diligently required of al the matiers contened in the bill mynystred by the parties, he saith he can no thing depose, save he saith that on Tywesday sevenyght next after Mighelmasse day last passid this man sworne was hired by Radeford to sette vppe a porche atte the south dore of his halle atte Uppecote and was come thider right be tyme, and yit er that he come Radeforde was ridyng to my lorde of Deuenshire, that tyme beyng atte Tydecombe, as Radefordis wife tolde him, and aboute xj or xij of the clok the same day before none he sawe Radeford come home ayeyn the same way fro Tyuerton ward, and was atte home atte dyner and all the day after, and the morne vppon, that is to say the Wandisday, he wente on huntyng for the

16. Crediton.

fox to a place callede Wolfridisworthi, and the Thursday al day he was atte home and the Friday til vij of the bell, and that day and tyme he toke his way to Londonward. More <he> cannought say. Al this he deposith of his verrey knowelege and sight. He is nought corrupte by price ne preyer, as he saith.

Thomas Skynner, taill*our* of the parissh of Poughill, the age of l wynter, sworne, examyned and diligently required of all the matiers contened in the bill mynystred by the parties, he saith he can no thing depose, savyng he saith that on Wandisday next afore Palmesonday was twelmonth he come to Exceter to visite two children of John Wolston whiche had bene with him afore atte foustre and were remeued to Exceter for the pestilence, that Wandisday he dyned with Radeford in North gate Strete and sone after mete aboute evensongtyme he rode with Radeford to his place called Uppecote. Examyned of the Thursday next folowyng, he saith that Radeford was at home atte his owen house atte Uppecote and that same day this man sworne soped with Radeford atte Uppecote. Examyned of the Monday next after Mighelmas day last passid, he saith of his verrey knowelege and sciens that Radeford was atte his owen place called Uppecote alle that day[17], for that day the tanenterie made clene the mylne lete, and was ther with ham walkyng with a splete staffe in his hande. As for Tywesday, Wandisday and Thursday he cannought depose, savyng bi the speche of his neghtbours whiche saith that he was atte home. More can he nought say of the matier contened in the bill. He is nought corrupte, as he saith.

Thomas Payne, carpenter of Crewis Morchard, the age of xl wynter and more, sworn, examyned and diligently required of all the matiers contened in the bill, he accordith in all thing with Richard Isaak sworne before. He is naught corrupte, as he saith.

[m. 5]

Sir John Michell, <prest>, annueller in the cathedrall chirche of Exceter, the age of l^ti wynter, sworne, examyned and diligently required vppon all the matier contened in the bill mynystred by the parties, he saithat bitwixte Ester and Wytsonday now was a

_____

17. 'for that day' struck out.

twelmonth, what day in certeyn he cannought depose, that William Tremayn beyng at Exceter afore a mannys hous of the same toune called Benet Skynner saide to this man sworne in this wise: 'Sir John, ye haue oftentymes saide that I haue no livelode, but now I haue that I haue soughte fore many day.' 'What is that?' quod he. 'Lo Sir, here is a dede that my fader hath yeve me the maner of North Hewissh!', and toke him the dede to rede, and he radde hit fro worde to worde. And whanne he had over radde hit, in a plite of the dede he *per*ceyued that one had amendid hit in certeyn mynymes with blak ynk, for the dede self was writon with caduke ynke. And then this preste sworne askid of this same William: 'Who has blakkid the mynymes?' 'For sothe', saide he, 'hit was almoste oute and I haue amendid hit my self.' Examyned wherwith that dede was sealid, he saith with rede wexe, and imprintid depe with a scalob. Examyned what date that dede bare, he cannought depose in certeyn, but he supposeth ten yeer afore that. It*em* this prest axkid William: 'Where haddist thow this dede?' 'For sothe', saide he, 'my faderis stiward brought hit me.' 'Who is that?' quod the prest. 'Mary, Sir', quod he, 'one Bithelake.' Examyned whether the axuns[18] of the seale were eny thing wette other defouled, he saith nay, also fer*re* as he *per*ceyved. More can he nought say of the matier contened in the bill. He is nought corrupte, as he saith.

Richard Orynge, taillour of the parissh of Seynt George of Exceter, the age of xxx[ti] wynter and more, sworn, examyned and duly required vppon all the matiers contened in the bill mynystred by the parties, he saithe he can no thing depose. Examyned if he wist or sawe Radeford in his house the Thursday other Friday next afore Palme Sonday was twelmonth, he saith in vertu of his sacramente he knewe him nought ther, also fer as he canne remember him. He is nought corrupte, as he saith.

John <u>alias</u> Janyn Husset, skynner of the parissh of Seynt George of Exceter, the age of xxv wynter, sworne, examyned and diligently required of alle the matiers contened in the bill mynystred by the parties, he saith that he can no thing depose, but he saith that divers *per*sones favoryng to Thomas Tremayn, as Benet Skynner, John Watte, William Tremayn, Philip Yerle, Geffrey Turpyn and

---

18. The reading of the MS is unclear: the word may be intended to be corrected to 'aguns'.

meny other mo, were with this man sworne to pray him and induce him that he shulde say that he sawe Radeford atte Exceter at Richard Taillo*ur* is house the Friday next afore Palme Sonday was twelmonth, and profered him xx s., and som of ham saide hit shulde be worth to him an hundreth shillyng*es*, and one of ham toke him in his hande meny grotes, how meny he wote never, but he supposith to the su*m*me of a noble, and he refusid all and saide he wolde nought be forsworne. He is nought corrupte by preyer ne price, as he saith.

William Butte, taillour of the parissh of Poughill, the age of xxvj^{ti} wynter, sworn, examyned and diligently required of all the matiers contened in the bill mynystred bi the parties, he saith of his verrey sciens and knowelege that Radeforde remeved fro his place of Uppecote and come to Exceter into a place in Cory Lane for the pestilence, and for so moche as his panter shulde abide stille atte Uppecote with his meyne ther, he prayed this man sworne to be with hym atte Exceter for a tyme, and so he was with him atte Exceter in Corylane in his office in his panterye vnto the Monday in the secunde weke of clene Lente was a twelmonth, and then he remeued oute of Corylane into Northgate Strete to Uptons house, and ther he contynewid his houshold vnto the Wandisday next afore Palme Sonday was twelmonth, and that Wandisday after mete he rode home to Uppecote and there abode that nyght the morne, the Thursday, and the Friday next after he come to Exceter ayein after none. Examyned what he can say of the Monday next after Mighelmasse day last passid, this man sworne saith that Radeford was atte home atte Uppecote alle that day, and the Tywesday next vppon Radeford rode to my lord of Deuenshire to Tydecomb and come ayen to his mete aboute xij of the clok, as he supposith, and abode atte home alle that day after. And on Wandisday next after he wente on huntyng, and the Thursday next vppon he was atte home alle day, and on Friday til vij of the clok in the mornyng, and then he toke his iourney to Londonward. Otherwise ne more can he nought depose in al the matiers contened in the saide bill. He is nought corrupt, as he saith.

John Toker, of the parissh of Poughill, toker, the age of xxx^{ti} wynter and more, sworne, examyned and diligently required of alle the matiers contened in the bill mynystred bi the parties, he cannought say, but he saith that the first weke in clene Lente was a twelmonth, as he supposith, the sessions were atte Exceter, and the next weke after the sessions were atte Launceston, atte whiche sessions was Nicholas Radeford and this man sworne with him, and the mene tyme Radefordis wife remeued ther household oute of Cory Lane into Northgate Strete to Upton is place, and when the sessions were done atte Launceston, he come home to Exceter and this man sworne with him, and fonde his wife and his household in the saide Northgate Strete. Examyned of the Thursday and Friday next afore Palme Sonday was twelmonth, he saith he can nought depose, for he saith he was that tyme atte London. Examyned of the Monday next after Mighelmasse day last passed, he saith of his verrey knowelege and sight that Nicholas Radeford was atte home atte his place atte Uppecote that same Monday, and ther he spake with him aboute viij of the clok afor none, and the cause of his comyng thider was to haue spokyn with Wolston, and so he dede, and wente with the saide Wolston to Morchard that same day[19] afore mete, and come ayein to Uppecote atte metis tyme, and after mete the same Monday Wolstone wente to Braderiche to holde courte ther, and Radefordis clerk with him and this man sworne also. And the Tywesday next folowyng this man sworne come afore the sonne risyng to Uppecote to ride with Wolston to Sir John of Dynham, that tyme beyng atte Herford[20] in Deuenschire, and as he was come to Uppecote, he sawe Radeford on horsebak to ride and speke with mi lord of Deuenshire at Tydecomb, and that same nyght Wolston come home to soper to Uppecote and this man sworne with him, and ther he sawe Nicholas Radeford sittyng atte the soper, and ferthermore he saith that he was with Nicholas Radeford atte Uppecote the Wandisday[21] and Thursday folowyng, and the Friday next vppon he rode with Nicholas Radeford in the mornyng to Sir William Palton is place called Lomene to Londonward, and ther a bode to mete, and the morne after he departid fro him and come home ayen. He is nought corrupte, as he saith.

John Coteler, somtyme mayer of Exceter, the age of xl wynter and more, sworne, examyned and diligently required of al the matiers contened in the bill mynystrid bi the parties, he cannought depose, saue onely he saith that on Monday or Tywesday next

19. MS say.
20. Harpford.
21. 'and Thursday 'struck out.

afore Passion Sonday was twelmonth he mette with Nicholas Radeford at Seynt Petris chirche of Exceter afore mete and bade him good morne, and saide: 'Sir, hit is saide me that ye be remeued oute of Cory Lane into North gate strete', and he saide ayen: 'Wist ye ne rather that?' and he said no, and then saide he that he wolde come and drynke with him after none, and so he dede, and Sir John Wolston with him, and fonde him ther, his wife and his household, and dranke with ham, and the mene tyme come in Sir James Richard and Sir John Fouler, vicares of the close of Exceter, and ferthermore he prayed Radeford to lene him an horse to ride ayenste my lorde of Glouceter, as he was comyng oute of Cornewale, and he lente him two hors and his man. He is nought corrupt, as he saith.

Sir Piers Wynterborn, prest, parson of Whitston, xxx[ti] wynter of age and more, sworne, examyned and diligently required of alle the matiers contened in the bill mynystrid by the parties, he saith he can no thing depose, saue onely he saith on Monday next after Mighelmasse day last passid he was with my Lady Palton atte Kirton[22] alle nyght, and the morne vppon, that is to say the Tywesday, atte Copleston is place atte dyner, and after none they rode toward Tyuerton by Radefordis place called Uppecote, and Radeford and his wife prayed this said ladi Palton to come in and drynke, and so they dede, and whan they had done Radeford sente a man with an horse to teche the saide ladie and hir maynye the way toward Tyuerton, and this he deposith of his verrey sight and knowelege. Examyned what tyme of the day hit was that my saide ladie shulde dryng with Radeford, he saith as he supposith betwixt ij and iij after none the said Tywesday. He is nought corrupte, as he saith.

William Batyn, toker of the parissh of Seynt David in the suburbis of Exceter, the age of xx wynter, sworn, examyned and diligently required of alle the matiers and articlis contened in the bill mynystred by the parties, he saith he can nothing depose, savyng he saith that on Monday next afore Ester that last was he was hired by the day iourney with one Richard Wode, toker, dwellyng in Seynt Sidewillis parissh, the whiche Richard saide to this man sworne and to his felawe: 'Sires', quod he, 'I have no

22. Crediton.

werk for yow to morne, never the lees, if ye will be rulid, you shall eyther of yow gete xij d. to morne and I shal pay yow my selfe'. 'Mary', saide this man sworne, 'I wolde fayne gete xij d., and I wist how in trouth'. Then saide Richard Wode: 'Ye shal bothe go to morne to Seynt Petris with Speke and Tremayn and say as they wol infourme yow.' Then saide this man sworne: 'Shall we be sworne ther to say the sothe?' 'For sothe', saide the saide Richard Wode, 'ther wil be an hundreth to morne that wol say as Speke and Tremayn wol say, and of al tham peravento*ur* ther shal nought be sworne but foure or fyve, and therfor ye may be wellynough ther and saye as other men sayen, and therfor be thow nought agast, for ther wol be thi fader, Piper, Skynner, Thomas Cosyn and other men.' And the morne after William Tremayn mette with this man sworne atte the Est yeate, and he saide to William Tremayn: 'God gif yow good morne, maister.' 'Sir,' quod this man sworne, 'Philip Yerle tolde me that I shulde haue money of yow.' 'Trewely', saide Tremayn, 'I wolde fayne take the money, but atte this tyme I haue nought a peny in myne purse, for I haue delyuered al my money.' 'Mary, Sir', quod this man sworne, 'and I had money, I couthe gete iij or iiij felawis to say like as Speke and Tremayn wol say.' 'By my trouth', quod he, 'bring me the iiij felawis, and thow shalt haue a noble for thi labo*ur*.' Then William Tremayn toke him by the honde and ladde him to Philip Yerlis dore, and the saide Tremayn askid of the saide Philip if he had eny money, and he saide nay, for he had bestowid hit like as he bede him. Then come oute this Philip oute of his house, and wente with this man sworne til on Lyndis house in the parissh of Seynt Paule to haue receyvid money ther, and when they were come thider, this Philip Yerle saide to this man sworne: 'My lorde is nought with in, go thi way and gete thi men and thow shalt be trewely payed, I shall undertake therfor.' Forthermore, this man beyng present in Seynt Petris chirche a fore the ymage of Seynt Petre callid 'the olde Petre' with other company brought to be sworne in Tremaynes side, herd with his eris William Tremayn say: 'Say thow that Radeford was here in the Monday, and thow the Tywesday,' and atte last he smote this man on the bak and said: 'Say thow the Wandisday,' and gen*e*rally saide: 'Alle ye that ben of the North gate quarter, say ye that ye sawe him here the Monday, and ye that ben in the High Strete towardis the Est yeate, say ye

[m. 6]

on the Tywesday, and ye with oute the Est yeate, say ye on the Wandisday.' And thus the saide William Tremayn departid the dayes amongis his witnesse. Afterward, vppon a Wandisday next afore Ester last passid, this man sworne was in his fadris house in the parissh of Seynt Pancrace, and ther was his fader, callede John Batyn, toker, Thomas Cosyn, sadeler, and other, and thider come Philip Yerle, wever, and bade ham be atte Seynt Petris alredie ayenst ix of the clok, and they sayed they wold. Never the les saide they: 'Let vs drynk ons or we go.' And then the saide Philip drewe oute of his sleve a gloue with money, and of that glove he toke a peny to sende for mede and ale, and saide by the faith of his bodie he had wared iiij mark*es* oute of that glove sithen hit was to nyght son sette. 'Ne force', quod Thomas Cosyn, 'thow hast deservid in this bargayn xx s. and x.' And then come Tremayn to the saide John Batyn stall and saide: 'Haue done sires', quod he, 'and com hens, for Radeford is come in atte Northgate strete with xl bonde churles and mo, whiche dar say none other than he woll.' And then after this man sworne is fader askid of this man whether he had fonge eny money in this matier, and he saide nay. And then saide his fader: 'Loke that thou fange or thow go.' Then he axed of his fader: 'Haue ye fonge money?' 'For sothe', quoth he, 'I haue fonge xl d. for me and my man.' And then saide he to his fader: 'Bewar fader, for ye moste be sworne whether ye haue fonge other no.' And then this man sworne wente to Radeford and diskeuered their counsel, and also sone as his fader and his felawship had aspied hit, the saide Thomas Cosyn come to this man sworne and saide: 'Thou ert a fals traytour, for thow hast deskivered our counsel. Be war go hens, for Sir John Speke wil kil the wher eu*er* he may take the.' He is nought corrupt, as he saith.

Richard Ree, smyth of the parissh of Seynt Laurence, sworne, examyned and diligentely required vppon the articles and matier contened in the bill mynystred by the parties, he saith he can no thing depose, saue onely ther that hit is surmyttid in the saide bill that Nicholas Radeford shuld haue bene atte Exceter the Thursday next afore Palme Sonday was twelmonth, he saith nay, also fer as he knowith. Examyned also of the Friday and Satirday folowyng, he saith he cannought depose of his presence nor of his absence. Examyned ferthermore if he sawe Nicholas Radeford atte Exceter the Tywesday sevenyght after Mighelmasse day that last was, he saith that he sawe Nicholas Radeford atte Exceter, whether hit was that Tywesday redely he wote never, wel he wote aboute that tyme he sawe him as he saith. Examyned if eny of the parties haue geuen him or promysid him eny good, he saith that one Jak Watte, taillo*ur*, come to this man sworne and said vnto him in this wise: 'I pray the that thow woldist come to Seynt Petris chirche and say to the co*m*missaries that thow sawest Radeford ride' by thi dore the Tywesday²³ sevenyght after Mighelmasse day.' Than saide this man sworne: 'For sothe, I reme[m]bre²⁴ me noght what day I sawe him, whethir hit was that day or no, I wote noght.' Than the said John Watte said: 'And thow wilt come and say that thow sawe Radeford ride by thi dore the saide Tywesday, I shal yeue the for this palotte ij s., nought withstondyng that I boughte hit of the afore tyme for xiiij d., for lettyng of thi werk.' And this man wolde nought ther of. Also this man sworne saith that the said Jak Watte said to him that he him self had i bought a payr of sporis of Richard Sporio*ur* of Exceter in the same maner wyse for to bere wittenesse that Nicholas Radeford was atte Exceter the said Tywesday. Also this man sworne saith that on John Ree saide to him that he had receyued xl d. for to come with Tremayn and depose for him atte Seynt Petris chirche. He is nought corrupte, as he saith.

John Bate, toker of the parissh of Seynt Dauid with oute the north²⁵ yeate of Exceter, the age of l wynter and more, sworne, examyned and diligently required vppon alle the matiers contened in the bill mynystrid by the parties, saith that he can no thing depose, savyng he saith that one Philip Yerle came to him to his wyndowe with oute North yeate, and axed of him whether he saw Radeford come to Exceter the Monday next after Mighelmasse last passid, and he saide nay, he sawe him nought. Tho saide Philip Yerle that he had sette a warante with Nicholas Radeford that day in the toune of Exceter forto areste William Tremayn, and: 'If thow wolt come and bere wittenesse that thow sawist Nicholas Radeford come ridyng in to the toune that day, thow shalt be rewardid also moche, as all thi tokyng wol be worth this weke.' And then saide this man sworne: 'For sothe, I wol nought bere

---

23. 'ty' faded and over an erasure.
24. MS 'remebre'.
25. MS 'northt'.

wittenesse of that I knowe nought.' He is nought corrupte, as he saith.

Nicholas Trenewith, skynner of the parissh of Seynt Stephenes, the age of xxiiij[ti] wynter, sworne, examyned and diligently required of all the matier contenid in the bill mynystred bi the parties, he saith he can no thing depose in the matier, save onely that William Tremayn and Philip Yerle come to him in a day in the Lente before Ester last was, and axed of this man sworne whether he wolde serne eny money. And he said: 'Ye, ful fayne'. And then said they if he wold come to Seynt Petris chirche the morne after and say as other men wold say, he and an hundreth mo, he shuld haue xx d. for his labo*u*r. And then saide this man sworne: 'I trowe if I come thider, I shal be sworne on a boke to say the sothe, and p*er*aventur I shulde lese money therfor.' And then saide they: 'Care nought for hit, for my maister Speke shal be thy warant.' And then saide this man sworne that he wold noght therof. And then saide they that on the morne after they wolde come and speke with him more of the matier before ix of the bell, but they come nought ayen til on Sonday next after and that[26] Sonday come Philip Yerle to Seynt Stephenes chirche to this man sworne and saide: 'A man, whi ne haddist thow fange money!' And then saide this man sworne: 'I wote wel hit wer nought for me to fange eny.' And tho axid this man of the saide Philip: 'What money haue ye delid?' And the said Philip answerde and saide: 'By God we haue delid x li. amongis ous.' He is nought corrupte, as he saith.

John Tracy of the parissh of Tuu*er*ton, the age of xxiiij wynter, sworne, examyned and diligently required of alle the matiers contened in the bill ministrid bi the parties, he saith he can no thing say, saue onely on Monday next after Mighelmasse day last passid he was sente in message to Nicholas Radeford fro my lorde of Deuenshire and fande Nicholas Radeford atte soper in his place atte Uppecote, and abode ther al nyght and lay in the same chamber that Frere Courteys lay in. And in the mornyng arly, that is to say the Tywesday, the saide Nicholas Radeford his clerk and this man sworne rode to Tyu*er*ton and so furth to Tydecomb to my lord of Deuenshire, and whan he had spoke with my saide lorde and brokyn his faste, he toke his leue and rode home ayein

26. MS 'the that'.

the fornone. The morne vppon, that is to say the Wandisday, this same man sworne spake with Nicholas Radeford in the parissh of Poughill a litil fro Uppecote, wher he was huntyng, in message fro my maister Botreaux, and ther spake with Wolstone. Other wise can he nought depose. He is nought corrupte by preyer ne price, as he saith.

William Wykier, constable of the hundreth of Colyton, the age of xxx^ti wynter and more, sworne examyned and diligently required vppon alle the matiers contened in the bill mynystrid bi the parties, saith that he can no thing depose, savyng that he saith that he rode with one Roger Wyke, brother in lawe to Nicholas Radeford, the Monday next after Mighelmasse day last passid to a place of the saide Nicholas called Uppecote and was ther al nyght with the saide Roger Wyke, Nicholas Radeford beyng present. And the morne vppon, that is to say the Tywesday, the saide Radeford rode to my lord of Deuenshire and come home ayein to his dyner aboute xij of the clok, as he supposith, and that nyght this man sworne come to Exceter with the saide Roger Wyke and was ther al nyght. He is nought corrupte, as he saith.

Benet Drew, mayer of Exceter, the age of l wynter and more, sworne, examyned and diligently required of all the matier contened in the bill mynystrid by the parties, he saith that he can no thing in esspecial depose, savyng he bryngith in a munynent sealid with the seal of the mayeraltie of Excetre and divers other sealis, like as hit apperith by the saide munyment, the whiche munyment he bringeth in writon in Latyn, sayng that alle that is contened in the munyment fro siche a clause reherced in the saide munyned 'Venit Benedictus Drew maior etc.' is tr[ewe][27] poynt to poynt in to the ende of the saide munyment, savyng he doutith him of a worde contened in the munyment weltoward the ende [...][28], whether that worde was saide other no, he remembrith him nought. Whiche munyment we sende yow annectid to this present exa[minacion][29]. Examyned forthermore if William Tremayn wer manasshid by eny creature to say other wise then hit was in his fre liberte, he saith nay by the othe[30] that he hath made. He saith that

27. MS damaged.
28. Damage to MS.
29. Damage to MS.
30. MS othe othe.

he said to him and comfortid him that he shulde nought spare for no man to say the treuthe, for he shulde haue fre goyng and fre comyng. Examyned ferthermore if he sawe or wist Radeford take to William Tremayn an hundreth nobles vppon a tippet, he saith by the vertu of his sacramente that he nether se ne herd no money proferd to him, ne no word spokyn ther of. More [can][31] he nought depose then he hath saide afore. He is noght corrupte, as he saith, by preyer ne price.

John Kyrton, citiner of Exceter, receyver of the Kynges Writtis, the age of xxx[ti] wynter and more, sworne, examyned and diligently required vppon alle th[e][32] matiers contened in the bill mynystred by the parties, acordith in alle his deposicion with the forsaide Benet Drew aboue examyned. He is nought cor[rupt][33], as he saith.

Vincent Hert, one of the stiwardis of the citee of Exceter, the age of xl wynter, sworne, examyned and diligently required vppon alle the matiers cont[ened][34] in the bill mynystred by the parties, acordith in all and singuler with Benet Drew afore examyned. He is nought corrupte, as he saith.

[rot. 3
m. 1]

Inquisicio et testium examinacio ex parte Nicholai Radeford et Rogeri Champernon productorum coram venerabili patre et domino, domino Edmundo, Exoniensis Episcopo, Magistris Johanne Cobethorn, ecclesie cathedralis beati Petri Exoniensis Decano, necnon et Waltero Colles, dicte ecclesie Precentore, excellentissimi in Christo principis et domini nostri domini Henrici dei gracia Regis Anglie et Francie et domini Hibernie Commissarijs in hac parte sufficienter et legittime deputatis, habite et facte in domo Capitulari ecclesie cathedralis Exoniensis antedicte, capella beate Marie virginis et loco Consistoriali infra dictam ecclesiam situatis certis diebus, videlicet a primo die Mensis Aprilis Anno domini Millesimo quadringentesimo Tricesimo nono vsque in

31. Margin of MS torn off.
32. Damage to MS.
33 Damage to MS.
34. Damage to MS.

deci*m*um diem Mensis Julij extunc p*roximo* sequent*em* Indiccione se*cun*da Pontific*atus* s*an*ctissimi in Ch*rist*o patris et domini n*ost*ri domini Eugenij diuina p*r*ouidencia p*a*pe quarti anno nono.

[*Inquisition and examination of witnesses produced for the part of Nicholas Radford and Roger Champernon before the venerable father and lord, the Lord Edmund, Bishop of Exeter, and Masters John Cobethorn, Dean of the cathedral church of St. Peter of Exeter, and Walter Colles, precentor of the said church, commissioners of the most excellent prince in Christ and our lord, the Lord Henry, by the grace of God King of England and France and Lord of Ireland, sufficiently and legitimately deputed in that part, taken and made in the chapter house of the aforesaid cathedral church of Exeter, the chapel of the Blessed Virgin Mary, and the consistorial place within the said church, on certain days, that is to say from 1 April 1439 to 10 July then next, in the second indiction, and the ninth year of the pontificate of the most holy father in Christ and our lord, the Lord Eugenius IV, by divine providence pope.*]

Thomas Courtenay, erle of Deuynshire, the age of xxvj wynter, examyned and diligentely required of alle the matiers contenyd in the billis mynystred bi Thomas Tremayn on that on parties and Nicholas Radeford and Roger Champernon on that other partie, saith that he can no thing depose of the saide matiers, savyng he saith that on Tywesday atte nyght next afore Palme Sonday was twelmonth he was at his maner of Colcomb and ther with him was Roger Champernon, and the morne vppon, that is to saye the Wandisday, Thursday and Friday next folowyng, til he had etc. Forthermore he saith that on Tywesday was sevenyght next after Mighelmas day last passid he was atte a place in Deuonshire callid Tydecomb with his moder and he sente for Radeford to come speke with him ther that day, and that same day afore none Radeford come to him to the saide place atte Tydecomb and spake with him, and after longe co*mm*unicacion he toke his leve and saide that he wold ride home to his place called Uppecote, and after none the same day my lord comyng fro his huntyng mette with Sir William Palton is wife, the whiche saide that she had bene that tyme with Radeford atte his place of Uppecote and ther drank with him. Otherwise can he nought depose, as he saith.

John Botreaux, squyer, the age of xlviij wynter and more, examyned and diligently requyred vppon alle the matiers mynystred by the parties, saith that he can no thing depose savyng he saith that on Monday next after Mighelmas day last passid he sente for Radeford by William Michell, his man, and after none the same day he sente for the saide Radeford by John Knoudiston, his man, and the morne vppon, as was the Tywesday sevenyght next after Mighelmas day that last was, he sawe Nicholas Radeford with my lord of Deuonshire atte Tydecombe besidis Tyuerton and spak with him of many divers matiers before metis tyme, and whan the saide Nicholas had done with my lord of Deuonshire he toke his leue and saide that he wold go to his house atte Uppecote. More can he nought depose. He is nought corrupte, as he saith.

[m. 2]

Olyver Hewyssh, gentilman dwellyng with Sir William Palton, knyght, age of xxvij yeer and more, sworne examyned and diligently required vppon alle the matier contened in the bill mynystred by the parties, he saith he can no thing depose, savyng onely he saith that he was at Nicholas Radefordis hous called Uppecote with my Lady Palton the Tywesday sevenyght next after Mighelmas day last passid, aboute iij of the belle after none, and ther the saide Ladie Palton and this man sworne, hir seruand, drank and disportid ham with Nicholas Radeford and his wife, they both beyng ther present. And after that the saide ladie and this man sworne and other of hir maynye toke hire leue of the saide Radeford and his wife and rode in their way to ward Tyuerton and so furth to hir owen place callede Uplomon. He is nought corrupte, as he saith.

Thomas Polbelle, yeman duellyng with Sir William Palton, knyght, the age of l wynter, sworne examyned and diligently required of all the matier and articles contened in the bill mynystrid bi the parties, accordith fro worde to worde in all his deposicion with Olyver Hewissh aboue examyned. He is nought corrupt, as he saith.

John Shillyngford, gentilman, the age of l wynter and more, sworne, examyned and diligentely required vppon alle the matiers mynystred by the parties, saith that in alle thing conteyned in the writyng mynystred to the commissaries by the mayer of Exceter acordith in alle wise as the mayer of Exceter hath deposed before.

Forthermore examyned if Radeford profered eny money to William
Tremayn and told hit vppon a tippet, as hit is surmytted in the
bill, he saith by the vertu of his sacrament that alle the tyme that
Radeford was in his hous this man sworne and he departid neu*er*
ne Radeford spake with no man pryvely, but openly that euere
man that was ther myght wel here him. And he nether herd ne sawe
Radeford profere Tremayn ne money, ne none was spoke of alle
that tyme by the sacrament that he made, as he saith. Examyned
forthermore if Radeford manasthed the said Tremayn to sende him
to pryson, he saith nay, but spak with him also faire as he coutht.
He saith that William Tremayn saide that he desclaundered neu*er*
Radeford, ne saide no suche wordis of him. He saith that when
their com*m*unicacion was done this man sworne with Radeford to
the durre and brought him goyng and lefte Tremayn in his house
and come in to him agayn and com*m*unid with him a grete while
after. More canne he nought depose. He is nought corrupte, as he
saith.

Et Ego, Johannes Polyng clericus, Exonien*sis* dioc*esis* publicus
auc*torita*te ap*os*tolica notarius, *p*remissis omnib*us* et singulis
dum sic, vt *p*remittit*ur*, agerent*ur* et fierent sub annis d*omi*ni,
indiccione, pontificatu, mensib*us*, dieb*us* et loc*is* p*re*dict*is*, regni
vero Reg*is* Anglie Henrici sexti post conquestum septimodecimo,
*p*resens personalit*er* interfui eaq*ue* omnia et singula sic fieri vidi et
audiui, alijsq*ue* arduis occupatus negocijs p*er* alium fidelem scribi
feci, publicaui et de mandato d*i*ctor*um* ven*er*abiliu*m* virorum
in d*i*cte inquisicio*n*is et exa*m*inacionis negocio com*m*issarior*um*
necnon et ad rogatum d*i*ctar*um* parciu*m* in hanc publicam formam
redegi, signoq*ue* et no*min*e meis solitis et consuetis signaui rogatus
et requisitus in fidem et testimonium omnium premissorum.

*[And I, John Polyng, clerk, notary public by apostolic authority
of the diocese of Exeter, personally present have taken part in
the premises, all and singular, when they were, as aforesaid,
enacted and done under the aforesaid years of the lord, indiction,
pontificate, months, days and places, and in the seventeenth year
of the reign of Henry VI, king of England, after the conquest, and
have seen and heard them all and singular so done, and, occupied
with other important affairs, have caused them to be written by
another trustworthy man, have published them, and by the order*

of the said venerable men, commissaries in the business of the said inquisition and examination, and also by the request of the said parties, have put them in this public form, and signed them with my habitual and accustomed mark and name, asked and required for the credence and witness of all the premises.]

[Notarial mark of Polyng]

RELATED PROCEEDINGS

1. [c.1438] THOMAS TREMAYNE VS. ROGER CHAMPERNON AND WILLIAM TREMAYNE FOR FORGING TITLE DEEDS RELATING TO THE MANOR OF NORTH HUISH. PRO, C1/39/142

To the right reuerend fadyr in God, Byshop*p*
of Bathe – Chaunceller of Ingelond

Humbely besechith yov youre pore oratoure Thom*as* Tremayn, for as myche as Rogg*er* Chambernon and William Tremayn forgyd a false dede, by the wheche Nicholas Tremayn, fadyr of youre said bisecher, whoys sone and heyre he ys, sholde yeue and gr*au*nte vn to the said William Tremayn the man*ere* of Northhywyssh in the counte of Deuonshyre with thapurten*au*nce, to haue and to halde to the said William and to hys heyres en fee, and a nother dede, b[y] the wheche the said Nicholas sholde haue relessyd vn to the said William and to hys heyres all the ryght that he hadde in the said man*ere* and sholde haue bond hym and hys heyres to have warantyd the same man*ere* to the said William, hys heyres and to hys assignes, and other diu*er*se dedes and mynymentz, of the wheche oder dedes and mynymentz youre said bisecher may not have notyce therof, the wheche dedys and mynymentz the said Rogg*er* in many diu*er*se places hath pupplysshyd and rad, and also the wyche dedys and mynymentz the said Rogg*er* hath in hys possessyon, besychyng yov that the said Rogg*er* myght brynge forth the said dedys and mynymentz bi youre discrec*i*on to ben

cancelyd. Pleasith hitt vn to yov of youre goode grace to consydre
these premessys and graunte a wrytte directe vn to the said Rogger
to appere be fore oure souerayngn lord the kynge in his chauncerie
vppon a certayn payn and a^t certayn day by yov to ben lymyted,
to ben examyned vppon these premesses, for the loue of god and
in waye of charyte.

Pleg*ij* de *prosequendo*:   Robertus Courteys
                                    Johannes Warre

2. [TRIN. 1439] NICHOLAS RADFORD VS. SIR JOHN SPEKE FOR BREACH OF THE STATUTE OF MAINTENANCE. PRO, CP40/714, rot. 320

[*Nicholas Radford appears in the court of common pleas in person
and complains that Sir John Speke of Haywood broke the statute
of maintenance by sustaining a certain suit in the king's court
of the city of Exeter between Radford and Thomas Tremayne,
William Tremayne and John Bydelake over certain conspiracies
and trespasses done to Radford by the Tremaynes and Bydelake,
for the part of the said William and John. He did so on Thursday
after the Epiphany 17 Hen. VI (8 Jan. 1439) at Tiverton and on
Tuesday then next (13 Jan. 1439) at Exeter castle, and Nicholas
claims £4000 damages.*

*Speke protests that he is a kinsman of Alice, the wife of the said
John Bydelake, viz. son of John Speke, son of Margaret Speke,
daughter of Alice Wortham, sister of Thomas Milford, father of
Agnes Combe, mother of Richard Combe, father of the said Alice,
the wife of John Bydelake, and furthermore he is a fellow of the
society of Lincoln's Inn, and was retained as professional counsel
to the Tremaynes and Bydelake in the matter.*

*Radford responds that Speke is a layman and not learned in the
law, and says that on the said Thursday Speke went to Tiverton
and procured Thomas, earl of Devon, to support the said William
and John and to sustain the quarrel for their part, and he offered
to the earl £10 for his assistance, which he refused to take. And
on the said Tuesday Speke went to Exeter castle and incited one
Tilman Cok, goldsmith, to testify that Radford should have sent
to him by Roger Castell a forged signet similar to that of Nicholas*

Tremayne to repair and should have sealed with the same signet a false deed by which Nicholas Tremayne was supposed to have enfeoffed the said William Tremayne of the manor of North Huish, and Radford says that on account of his diffamation by the accusation of the forgery and of other trespasses and conspiracies hatched by the said Thomas Tremayne, William Tremayne and John Bydelake against him, he brought the said action in the Exeter mayor's court.

Speke says that the said Thomas Tremayne, William Tremayne and John Bydelake were given to understand that the said Nicholas Radford was with the earl of Devon offering to stand by his arbitration in the said quarrel if the earl would take it upon himself, on which grounds the said Thomas, William and John required Speke as their counsellor to go to the earl at Tiverton to inform him fully of the circumstances of the dispute and to offer for their part to submit to his arbitration, for which intent the earl was to have from the said Thomas, William and John the said £10 which the same John Speke offered to the earl. And he further says that that he was fully informed by the said William Tremayne and many other trustworthy men that the said Tilman had testified that the same William Tremayne and Roger Castell, Radford's clerk, offered to the said Tilman a badly made lead seal with an escallop to amend and because Tilman's sight on account of his age was not clear enough to amend it, he sent them to a certain Thomas Goldsmyth, his associate, to amend the seal better and more clearly, wherefor Speke examined Tilman in the guildhall of Exeter whether his testimony was true or not.]

Devon – Johannes Speke de Haywode in comitatu predicto miles in misericordia pro pluribus defaltis etc.

Idem Johannes attachiatus fuit ad respondendum tam domino Regi quam Nicholao Radeford de placito quare, cum in statuto apud Westmonasterium nuper edito contineatur quod nulla persona regni Regis Anglie, cuiuscumque status seu condicionis fuerit, aliquam querelam in patria nec alibi manuteneat seu sustentet sub pena imprisonamenti et faciendi Regi finem et redempcionem ad voluntatem suam, quelibet videlicet iuxta statum, gradum et demeritum sua, predictus Johannes querelam cuiusdam loquele que fuit in curia Regis civitatis Exonie coram maiore et ballivis eiusdem civitatis sine brevi Regis secundum consuetudinem civitatis predicte inter prefatum Nicholaum et Thomam Tremayn, Willelmum Tremayn et Johannem Bydelake, <de> quibusdam conspiracionibus et transgressionibus prefato Nicholao per prefatos Tho[mam], Willelmum et Johannem Bydelake illatis, ut dicitur, pro parte predictorum Willelmi et Johannis Bydelake apud Tuverton et castrum Ex[onie] manutenuit et sustentavit, in domini Regis contemptum et ipsius Nicholai grave dampnum ac contra formam statuti predicti et contra prohibicionem Regis etc. Et unde idem Nicholaus qui tam pro domino Rege quam pro se ipso sequitur in propria persona sua queritur quod, cum in statuto predicto contineatur quod nulla persona regni Regis Anglie, cuiuscumque status seu condicionis fuerit, aliquam querelam in patria nec alibi manuteneat seu sustentet sub pena imprisonamenti et faciendi domino Regi finem et redempcionem ad voluntatem ipsius domini Regis, quelibet videlicet iuxta statum, gradum et demeritum sua, predictus Johannes Speke querelam cuiusdam loquele que fuit in curia eiusdem Regis civitatis Exonie coram maiore et ballivis eiusdem civitatis sine brevi dicti domini Regis secundum consuetudinem civitatis predicte inter prefatum Nicholaum et predictos Thomam, Willelmum et Johannem Bydelake de quibusdam conspiracionibus et transgressionibus prefato Nicholao et prefatos Thomam, Willelmum et Johannem Bydelake illatis, ut dicitur, pro parte predictorum Willelmi et Johannis Bydelake die Jovis proximo post festum Epiphanie domini anno regni dicti domini Regis nunc decimo septimo apud Tuverton et die Martis extunc proximo sequente apud castrum Exonie manutenuit et sustentavit in ipsius domini Regis nunc contemptum et ipsius Nicholai grave dampnum ac contra formam etc. unde dicit quod deterioratus est et dampnum habet ad valenciam quatuor milium librarum. Et inde producit sectam etc.

Et predictus Johannes Speke in propria persona sua venit et defendit vim et iniuriam et quicquid etc. quando etc. Et protestando quod ipse est consanguineus Alicie, uxoris predicti Johannis Bydelake, videlicet filius Johannis Speke, filij Margarete Speke, filie Alicie Wortham, sororis Thome Milford, patris Agnetis Combe, matris Ricardi Combe, patris ipsius Alicie, uxoris Johannis Bydelake, pro placito dicit quod predictus Nicholaus accionem predictam versus eum habere non debet quia dicit quod ipse est et per duodecim annos ante predictos dies Jovis et Martis quibus supponitur manutenciones predictas fieri et ante levacionem querele predicte et tempore levacionis eiusdem querele ac ante manutenciones predictas suppositas et temporibus manutencionum illarum suppositarum fuit et adhuc est unus sociorum de societate hospicij vocati Lyncolnesyn in London' in parochia Sancti Andree Apostoli et warda de Faryngdon extra situati quod est et a diu fuit quoddam hospicium hominum de curia legis Anglie temporalis in quo tam ipse Johannes Speke, [quam] alij apprenticij in lege periti ac alij legem terre Anglie discentes et erudientes morantur et a tempore non modico morabantur, quodque ipse ante levacionem querele predicte et ante manutenciones predictas suppositas et temporibus manutencionum predictarum suppositarum fuit et adhuc est homo consiliarius de et in lege predicta eruditus et dicit quod ipse ad et per requisicionem predictorum Willelmi et Johannis Bydelake ac Thome Tremayn ante manutenciones predictas suppositas et post levacionem querele predicte retentus fuit apud Exoniam essendi de consilio predictorum Thome et Johannis Bydelake in materia querele predicte virtute cuius quidem retencionis idem Johannes Speke fuit [de] consilio predictorum Thome. Willelmi et Johannis Bydelake in eadem materia et prebuit eis inde consilium prout ei b[ene licuit], que est eadem manutencio de qua idem Nicholaus tulit accionem suam predictam. Et hoc paratus est ver[ificare et] petit iudicium si idem Nicholaus dictam accionem inde in hoc casu versus eum habere seu manutenere debet [etc.] Et predictus Nicholaus, protestando quod predictus Johannes Speke est laicus et de lege terre minime erudit[us, et] dicit quod ipse ab accione sua predicta versus ipsum Johannem Speke habenda per aliqua preallegata excludi [non debet], quia quo ad dictam manutencionem apud predictam villam de Tuverton factam idem Nicholas [dicit quod predictus] Johannes Speke dicto die Jovis quo etc. accessit ad eandem villam de Tuverton et adtunc et ibi[dem excitavit] et procuravit Thomam, comitem Devonie, ad auxiliandum, assistendum et supportandum predictos Willelmum Tre[mayn et] Johannem Bydelake versus ipsum Nicholaum im dicta querela necnon ad sustentandum querelam predictam pro parte Willelmi et Johannis Bydelake et optulit eidem comiti decem libras adtunc et ibidem pro auxilio, assistencia, [supportacione] et sustentacione suis predictis inde habendo, quas decem libras idem comes recipere recusavit. Et hoc paratus est verificare, unde petit iudicium et quod predictus Johannes Speke de manutencione illa convincatur et dampna ea occasione adiudicari etc. Et quo ad dictam manutencionem factam apud castrum predictum, idem Nicholaus dicit quod predictus Johannes Speke predicto die Martis quo etc. accessit ad idem castrum et tunc ibidem excitavit et procuravit quendam Tilmannum Cok, goldsmyth, ad testificandum et affirmandum versus ipsum Nicholaum quod ipse falso et fraudulenter quoddam signetum controfactum ad similitudinem signeti cusiusdam Nicholai Tremayn eidem Tilmanno ad emendandum apud Exoniam per Rogerum Castell mittere debuisset, et cum eodem signeto sigillasse debuisset quandam falsam cartam, per quam ipse Nicholaus Tremayn feoffasse debuisset prefatum Willelmum Tremayn de manerio de Northuwysshe cum pertinencijs in [modo] predicto, habendo sibi et heredibus suis imperpetuum, et idem Nicholaus dicit quod pro publicacione dictarum controfacture signeti predicti, sigillacionis carte predicte et conspiracione inde inter eos prehabita et facta in scandalum, obprobrium et infamiam nominis eiusdem Nicholai, ac pro alijs transgressionibus et conspiracionibus eidem Nicholao per predictos Thomam Tremayn, Willelmum et Johannem Bydelake apud Exoniam ante levacionem querele predicte illatis, idem Nicholaus Radeford dictam querelam in prefata curia

[*rot. 320d*] Exonie ante easdem manutenciones et temporibus earundem manutencionum secutus fuit, que omnia et singula idem Nicholaus paratus est verificare prout curia etc. unde petit iudicium et quod idem Johannes Speke de manutencione illa convincatur et dampna occasione manutencionis illius sibi adiudicari etc.

Et predictus Johannnes Speke quo ad manutencionem predictam suppositam apud predictam villam de Tuverton dicit quod datum fuit intelligi predictis Thome Tremayn, Willelmo et Johanni Bydelake quod predictus Nicholaus Radeford fuit cum prefato comite offerendo se ipsum stare in alto et basso arbitrio, ordinacioni et iudicio ipsius comitis de et super dicta accione unde querela predicta levata fuit in casu quo idem comes illud super se accipere voluisset, quo pretextu ijdem Thomas Tremayn, Willelmus et Johannes Bydelake requirebant ipsum Johannem Speke tanquam eorum consiliarium ad accedere predictam villam de Tuverton ad prefatum comitem ad ipsum de querela predicta et circumstancijs eiusdem plenius informandum et offerendum pro parte ipsorum Thome Tremayn, Willelmi et Johannis Bydelake quod ipsi se submitterent stare in alto et in basso ordinacioni et iudicio ipsius comitis de et super dicta accione unde querela predicta levata fuit pro quo intendendo idem comes haberet de ipsis Thoma Tremayn, Willelmo et Johanne Bydelake decem libras quas idem Johannes Speke predicto die Jovis adtunc et ibidem prefato comiti optulit prout ei bene licuit absque hoc quod idem Johannes Speke excitavit seu procuravit dictum comitem ad auxiliandum, assistendum et supportandum predictos Willelmum et Johannem Bydelake versus ipsum Nicholaum in dicta querela seu ad sustentandum querelam illam pro parte ipsorum Willelmi et Johannis Bydelake aut eorum alterius aut optulit eidem comiti dictas decem libras aut aliquem denarium inde pro auxilio, assistencia, supportacione et sustentacione suis predictis in querela predicta habendo prout dictus Nicholaus Radeford superius allegavit. Et hoc paratus est verificare unde petit iudicium et quod idem Nicholas ab accione sua predicta inde precludatur etc. Et quo ad dictam manutencionem suppositam factam fuisse apud castrum predictum idem Johannes Speke ulterius dicit quod ipse plene informatus fuit per predictum Willelmum Tremayn et alios quamplures fidedignos quod predictus Tilmannus expresse cognovit et testatus fuit quod idem Willelmus Tremayn ac Rogerus Castell clericus predicti Nicholai Radeford optulerunt eidem Tilmanno quoddam sigillum plumbeum cum uno *Scalop* in eodem sculpato non bene factum emendandum et quia visus eiusdem Tilmanni senio confracti non fuit clarus ad illud emendandum, idem Tilmannus ipsos misit cuidam Thome Goldsmyth, socio ipsius Tilmanni, ad sigillum illud melius et clarius emendandum per quod idem Johannes Speke in Guyhalda civitatis Exonie prefatum Tilmannum examinavit de cognicione et testimonio suis predictis utrum vera essent necne ad cognoscendum inde plenius veritatem absque hoc quod ipse excitavit seu procuravit ipsum Tilmannum ad testificandum vel affirmandum versus prefatum Nicholaum Radeford quod ipse falso et fraudulenter quoddam signetum controfactum ad similitudinem signeti dicti Nicholai Tremayn eidem Tilmanno ad emendandum in forma predicta mittere debuisset et cum eodem sigillo sigillasse debuisset aliquam falsam cartam prout idem Nicholaus Radeford superius versus eum allegavit. Et hoc idem Johannes Speke similiter paratus est verificare unde petit iudicium et quod predictus Nicholaus Radeford ab accione sua predicta inde precludatur etc.

Et predictus Nicholaus Radeford quo ad predictam manutencionem apud predictam villam de Tuverton factam dicit quod predictus Johannes Speke excitavit et procuravit prefatum comitem ad auxiliandum, assistendum et supportandum predictos Willelmum Tremayn et Johannem Bydelake versus ipsum Nicholaum Radeford in dicta querela, et ad sustentandum [q]uerelam illam pro parte ipsorum Willelmi et Johannis Bydelake et eidem comiti optulit dictas decem libras pro [a] uxilio, assistencia, supportacione et sustentacione suis predictis in querela predicta habendo modo et forma quibus [i]dem Nicholas Radeford versus ipsum allegavit. Et hoc petit quod inquiratur per patriam. Et predictus Johannes [S]peke similiter. Et quo ad dictam manutencionem apud castrum predictum factam predictus Nicholaus Radeford ulterius dicit quod predictus Johannes Speke excitavit et procuravit prefatum Tilmannum ad testificandum et affirmandum versus ipsum Nicholaum quod ipse falso et fraudulenter quoddam signetum ad similitudinem signeti predicti Nicholai Tremayn eidem Tilmanno ad emendandum mittere debuisset et cum eodem sigillasse debuisset cartam predictam modo et forma quibus idem Nicholaus Radeford superius versus eum similiter allegavit. Et hoc eciam ipse Nicholaus petit quod inquiratur per patriam. Et predictus Johannes Speke similiter. Ideo quo ad exitus huius placiti preceptum est vicecomiti quod venire faciat hic in Octabis Sancti Michaelis xij etc. per quos etc. Et qui nec etc. ad recognoscendum etc. Quia tam etc.

3. [JULY x NOV. 1439] SIR JOHN SPEKE VS. JAMES CHUDLEIGH, SHERIFF OF DEVON, JOHN KIRTON, HIS OFFICER, AND NICHOLAS RADFORD, FOR THE FRAUDULENT EMPANELLING OF A PARTIAL JURY. PRO, C1/45/236

The petition dates from after the inception of the suit in the court of common pleas printed above, and before the end of Chudleigh's shrievalty on 5 Nov. 1439.

To the reuerent fader in God, the Bisshopp
of Bathe, Chaunceller of Englond

Mekely beseketh your cotidian oratour John Speke of Deuenshire, knyght, that for asmych as an accion of maintenaunce was taken by oon Nicholas Raddeford, aduersarie vnto your seid besecher, vpon whiche accion an issu was ioyned and a venire *facias* for the retorne send vnto Jamys Chudelygh, sheryf of Deuenshire, and the seid retorne made by the seid sheryf and his officer, John Kirton of Excestre, your seid besecher hauyng warnyng of strange *p*ersones suche a retorne made, sued and send to the seid sheryf and his officer for a copie, and so a copie vnto your seid besecher was delyuered by the seid sheryf of xxiiij namys ryght worthy, which at your co*mm*aundement is redy to be shevved, the said sheryf fully promyttyng vnto your seid besecher in no wyse to varie ne chaunge it, but oonly the same to send into the court. And afterward the seid sheryf and his seid officer John Kirton <and Nicholas Radford> made a contrarie and a nevve retorne of xxxviij namys, of whiche the more partie been ful parciall and fauorable with the seid Nicholas Radeford and ennemys to your seid besecher, as by diu*er*s grete and notable menes it playnly appereth, hauyng in your g*r*acious lordship consideracion that on the seid accion the seid Nicholas Radeford, adu*er*sarie vnto your seid besecher, hathe declared vj^ml mark damage importable and vttermist vndoyng to your seid besecher of lesse then by your hiegh wysdome and g*r*acious lordshi*p* it be remedied, wherefore beseketh your seid besecher to graunte writtes sub pena to do make the seid Jamys Chudelygh, sheryf of Deuenshire, John Kirton, his officer, and Nicholas Radeford come byfore y*our* lordshi*p* and to be examined of al these greuaunces and causes of the chaunge of the seid retorne, and by your high wisdome this to be reformed, in the hiegh reu*er*ence of oure lord god and in the weye of charitee.

4. [1439x42] PETITION BY THOMAS TREMAYN TO THE KING AND LORDS IN PARLIAMENT CONCERNING THE UNLAWFUL SEIZURE BY THOMAS COURTENAY, EARL OF DEVON, OF THE MANOR OF RAKE. PRO, SC8/345/E1319

The petition may either have been presented during the parliament of 1439–40, which assembled just over a week after the earl's supposed incursion into Rake and was dissolved the following February, or during that of 1442.

To the kyng our sou*er*aign Lord and to the full discrete Lordes of this *p*resent parlement assembled

Besecheth mekely your pouer and contynuell oratour, Thomas
Tremayn of Deven shire, that where Nicholas Tremayn his fadir,
whose heir he is, was seised peasibely of the Maner of Rake with
the appurtenaunce in the shyre abouesaid in his demesne as in fee
and therof died seised, aftir whose dethe the said Thomas entred in
to the said maner and thereof was seised vn to the tyme that nowe
late your said besecher by Thomas Erle of Devenshire the iij^de day
of Nouembre the yere of your noble Reigne the xviij was therof
wrongfully put oute and disceysed wherupon your said besecher
many tymes and ofte to his importable costes and charges in the
mooste louly wise suyd to þe said Erle and his counsaill that it
myght like his goode Lordeship to considre the possessioun right
and title of your said besecher in these premisses and therupon
that his said possessioun title and Right myght be seien examyned
and demeaned bi his counsaill and by such counsaill of your said
besecher as might pleese his Lordship whereupon the possessioun
right and title of your said besecher was duely examyned and
founde for him and that notwithstondyng the said Erle contynuelly
sith þe said disceison hath occupied the said maner and thereof
take the proufites and yet dothe and the howses, [...]¹ wodetrees
beyng in the said maner cutte falled down wasted and distroied
to þe vtter impouerisshyng of your said besecher. Please it your
moost speciall grace the premisses graciously to considre and the
grete myght birthe and alia[unce of]² the said Erle in the parties of
Devenshire and that moost partie of the gentlesse of the said shire
be his homagers and tenauntz ageyns whom your seid besecher by
the couyrs of your lawe of this your noble Reaume by assise entre
ne oth[...]³ the said shyre for the causes afore rehersed myght not
ne durste not sue ne entre in his said maner for to commaunde
the said Erle beying nowe here at this presente parlement to
appere afore you and your counsaill daily and ther to a[nswer to
the pre]misses⁴ and to be examyned therof so that Right may be
done to your said besecher and that the said Erle haue straitely
in commaundement vpon his liegeaunce or vpon a notable peyne

1.   Damage to MS.
2.   Damage to MS.
3.   Damage to MS.
4.   Damage to MS.

that he departe not fro this present p*a*rlement [until the]⁵ matier be examyned and dete*r*myned by you and your said counsaill or by such of your Justices as it may please your hieghnesse for the love of god and in way of charitee.

5.   Damage to MS.

GLOSSARY

anueller	a priest who celebrates anniversary masses for the dead
axid	asked
basillerd	basilard, a type of dagger
behight	(of behesten) promised
besecher	petitioner, supplicant
borwes	sureties, mainpernors
brasuter	brewer
caduke	fading
clok	clock
cloke	cloak
cordewayner	cordwainer, a shoemaker
cotidian	daily
counsaill	council, counsel
demeaned	judged
disceison	disseisin
disceyse	to disseise
durre	door
fangen	to receive, take
feoffee	a trustee of an individual's lands
ferrour	smith
foustre	to foster
gentlesse	gentry
greuaunce	grievance

homager	one owing homage to a lord
importable	unbearable
lekis	leeks
lene	lend
liegeaunce	allegiance
mark	reckoning unit of money, 13*s*. 4*d*.
mynymentz	muniments
mynymes	minims, the vertical strokes making up the letters i, u, m and n
neven	to mention
oratoure	petitioner, supplicant
panter	pantler, household official responsible for the pantry
parciall	partial, biased
peasibely	peacefully
rather	sooner
relece	to release
ruwellis	rowels, small wheels with radial points forming the extremity of a spur
sacrament	oath
shevve	to show
sith	since
sporis	spurs
staynour	painter or dyer
toker, touker	tucker, fuller
Twelmonth	a year (twelve months)
varie	alter, amend
vicaries	vicars choral (of Exeter cathedral)
webber	weaver
weder	weather

Street and place names:

Brode Yeate	Broadgate (to the cathedral close)
Calendrishay	Kalendarhay
Cory Lane	Corre Street
Goldsmithrew	Goldsmith Street

Waterbear street	Waterbeer Street
St Mary the More	St. Mary Major
Seynt Olauys parissh	St. Olave
Seynt Pancrace	St. Pancras
Seynt Paule chirche	St. Paul
Monkyn Sele	Zeal Monachorum
Northgate strete	North Street
Paule street	Paul Street
Carfoz	The Carfax
Lomene	Uploman
Yeldehal	guildhall

Feast and saints' days:

Mid-Lent Sunday	The fourth Sunday in Lent (Sunday before Passion Sunday)
Michaelmas day	29 September
Palm Sunday	Sunday before Easter
Passion Sunday	The fifth Sunday in Lent (Sunday before Palm Sunday)
Lammasse	Lammas day (1 August)

SELECT BIBLIOGRAPHY

I. MANUSCRIPT SOURCES

British Library, London
Additional Charters

Devon Record Office, Exeter

158M	Tremayne of Collacombe MSS
1718A/add./PW	Exeter, Holy Trinity parish, churchwardens' accounts
2946A-99/PW	Exeter, St. Petrock's Parish, churchwardens' accounts
3799M-0	Seymour of Berry Pomeroy MSS
5714M	Exeter deeds
Chanter XII (i)	Episcopal Register of George Neville
Chanter XII (ii)	Episcopal Registers of John Booth, Peter Courtenay, Richard Fox, Oliver King, Richard Redman and John Arundell
D1508M	Courtenay of Powderham MSS
Exeter city archives,	
	Mayor's Court Rolls
	Mayor's Tourn Rolls
	Receivers' Accounts

Exeter cathedral, Dean and Chapter Archives

2594/1
2595/12
2596/2
2596/4
2925/12
3550
5160
VC/3351

The National Archives: Public Record Office, Kew

C1	Court of Chancery, Early Chancery Proceedings
C4	Court of Chancery, Answers and Depositions
C47	Chancery, Miscellanea
C67	Chancery, Supplementary Patent Rolls
C139	Chancery, Inquisitions *post mortem*, Henry VI
C140	Chancery, Inquisitions *post mortem*, Edward IV
C241	Chancery, Certificates of Statute Merchant and Statute Staple
C242	Chancery, Certificates of Election of Coroners and Verderers
C244	Chancery, *Corpus cum Causa* Files
C254	Chancery, *Dedimus Potestatem* Files
C261	Chancery, Counterwrits
CP40	Court of Common Pleas, Plea (*De Banco*) Rolls
E13	Exchequer of Pleas, Plea Rolls
E101	Exchequer, Accounts Various
E122	Exchequer, Particulars of Customs Accounts
JUST1	Justices in Eyre, of Assize, of Oyer and Terminer, and of the Peace, Rolls and Files
KB9	Court of King's Bench, Ancient Indictments
KB27	Court of King's Bench, Plea (*Coram Rege*) Rolls
KB145	Court of King's Bench, *Recorda* files
KB146	Court of King's Bench, *Panella* files
SC1	Special Collections, Ancient Correspondence
SC6	Special Collections, Ministers' Accounts
SC8	Special Collections, Ancient Petitions

II. PRINTED PRIMARY SOURCES

Calendar of the Close Rolls (61 vols., London, H.M.S.O., 1892–1963).

Calendar of the Fine Rolls (22 vols., London, H.M.S.O., 1911–63).

Calendar of Inquisitions post Mortem (26 vols., London and Woodbridge, H.M.S.O. and The National Archives, 1896–2009).

Calendar of Papal Letters (14 vols., London, H.M.S.O., 1893–1960).

Calendar of the Patent Rolls (53 vols., London, H.M.S.O., 1891–1916).

The Chronicle of Exeter 1205–1722 ed. Todd Gray (Exeter, 2005).

Death and Memory in Medieval Exeter ed. David Lepine and Nicholas Orme (Exeter, Devon and Cornw. Rec. Soc. n.s. 47, 2003).

Exeter Freemen 1266–1967 ed. M.M. Rowe and A.M. Jackson (Exeter, Devon and Cornwall Record Soc. extra ser. i, 1973).

Inquisitions and Assessments relating to Feudal Aids (6 vols., London, 1899–1920).

Letters and Papers of John Shillingford, Mayor of Exeter, 1447–50 ed. S.A. Moore (London, Camden Soc. o.s. ii, 1871).

Registrum Thome Bourgchier Cantuariensis archiepiscopi, A.D. 1454–1486 ed. F.R.H. Du Boulay (Canterbury and York Soc. 54, 1957).

The Register of Edmund Stafford ed. F.C. Hingeston-Randolph (London, 1886).

The Register of Edmund Lacy ed. F.C. Hingeston-Randolph (2 vols., London, 109-15).

The Register of Edmund Lacy, Bishop of Exeter, 1420–1455 ed. G.R. Dunstan (5 vols., Torquay, 1963–72).

The Register of John Stafford, bishop of Bath and Wells, 1425–1443 ed. T.S. Holmes (2 vols., London, Som. Rec. Soc. xxxi-xxxii, 1915–16).

The Register of Nicholas Bubwith, bishop of Bath and Wells, 1407–1424 ed. T.S. Holmes, (2 vols., London, Som. Rec. Soc. xxix-xxx, 1914).

Rotuli Parliamentorum ed. J. Strachey (6 vols., London, 1783).

Statutes of the Realm (11 vols., London, 1810–28).

III. SECONDARY SOURCES

Attreed, Lorraine C., *The King's Towns. Identity and Survival in Late Medieval English Boroughs* (New York et al., 2001).

Baker, J.H. (ed.), *Legal Records and the Historian* (London, 1978).

Carpenter, Christine, *Locality and Polity* (Cambridge, 1992).

Cavill, P.R., *The English Parliaments of Henry VII, 1485–1504* (Oxford, 2009).

Cherry, Martin, 'The Courtenay Earls of Devon: The Formation and Disintegration of a Late Medieval Aristocratic Affinity', *Southern History*, i (1979), 71-97.

Cherry, Martin, 'The Crown and Political Community in Devonshire, 1377–1461' (Univ. of Wales, Swansea, Ph.D. thesis, 1981).

Cherry, Martin, 'The Struggle for Power in Mid-Fifteenth Century Devonshire', in *Patronage, the Crown and the Provinces in Later Medieval England* ed. R.A. Griffiths (Gloucester, 1981), 123-44.

Clark, Linda (ed.), *The History of Parliament: The Commons 1422–61* (forthcoming).

Curtis, M.E., *Some Disputes between the City and the Cathedral Authorities of Exeter* (Manchester, 1932).

Emden, A.B., *A Biographical Register of the University of Oxford* (3 vols., Oxford, 1957–59).

Fisher, J.H., 'Chancery and the Emergence of Standard Written English in the Fifteenth Century', *Speculum*, lii (1977), 870-99.

Fowler, R.C., 'Legal Proofs of Age', *EHR*, xxii (1907), 101-3.

Gibbs, Vicary *et al.* (eds.), *The Complete Peerage* (12 vols., London, 1910–59).

Haskett, T.S., 'Country Lawyers? The Composers of English Chancery Bills', in *The Life of the Law* ed. Peter Birks (London, 1993), 9-23.

Holford, Matthew, ' "Testimony (to some extent fictitious)": proofs of age in the first half of the fifteenth century', *Historical Research*, (forthcoming).

James, J.M., 'The Norman Benedictine Alien Priory of St. George, Modbury, AD c.1135–1480', *Transactions of the Devonshire Association*, cxxxi (1999), 81-104.

King, H.P.F., Jones, B., and Horn, J.M. (eds.), *Fasti Ecclesiae Anglicanae 1300–1541* (12 vols., London, 1962–67).

Kleineke, Hannes, 'The Commission *de Mutuo Faciendo* in the Reign of Henry VI', *EHR*, cxvi (2001), 1-30.

Kleineke, Hannes, ' "þe Kynges Cite": Exeter in the Wars of the Roses', in *Conflicts, Consequences and the Crown in the Late Middle Ages: The Fifteenth Century VII* ed. L.S. Clark (Woodbridge, 2007), 137-56.

Kowaleski, Maryanne, 'The Commercial Dominance of a Medieval provincial Oligarchy: Exeter in the late fourteenth century', *Mediaeval Studies*, xlvi (1984), 355-84, repr. in *The English Medieval Town: A Reader in Urban History 1200–1540* ed. Richard Holt and Gervase Rosser (1990), 184-215.

Kowaleski, Maryanne, *Local markets and Regional Trade in Medieval Exeter* (Cambridge, 1995).

Lega-Weekes, Ethel, 'The Pre-Reformation History of the Priory of St. Katherine, Polsloe, Exeter', *Transactions of the Devonshire Association*, lxvi (1934), 181-99.

Lega-Weekes, Ethel, 'The Hollands of Bowhill in St. Thomas's, Exeter', *Devon & Cornwall Notes and Queries*, xviii(7) (1935), 300-05.

Lepine, D.N., 'The Courtenays and Exeter Cathedral in the Later Middle Ages', *Transactions of the Devonshire Association*, cxxiv (1992), 41-58.

Maddern, P.C., *Violence and Social Order: East Anglia 1422–1442* (Oxford, 1992).

Martin, M.T., 'Legal Proofs of Age', *EHR*, xxii (1907), 526-27.

Myers, A.R., 'Parliamentary Petitions in the Fifteenth Century', *EHR*, lii (1937), 385-404, 590-613, repr. in *idem, Crown, Household and Parliament in Fifteenth-Century England*, ed. C.H. Clough, 1-44.

Myers, A.R., 'Some Observations on the Procedure of the Commons in Dealing with Bills in the Lancastrian Period', *University of Toronto Law Journal*, iii (1939), 51-73, repr. in *idem, Crown, Household and Parliament*, ed. Clough, 45-67.

Orme, Nicholas, 'The Medieval Clergy of Exeter Cathedral: I. The Vicars and Annuellars', *Transactions of the Devonshire Association*, cxiii (1981), 79-102.

Orme, Nicholas, 'Sir John Speke and his Chapel in Exeter Cathedral', *Transactions of the Devonshire Association*, cxviii (1986), 25-41.

Orme, Nicholas, 'Access and Exclusion: Exeter Cathedral, 1300–1540', in *Freedom of Movement in the Middle Ages* ed. Peregrine Horden (Donington, 2007), 267-86.

Radford, G.H., 'Nicholas Radford, 1385(?)–1455', *Transactions of the Devonshire Association*, xxxv (1903), 251-78.

Radford, G.H., 'The Fight at Clyst in 1455', *Transactions of the Devon Association*, xliv (1912), 252-65.

Radford, Ursula, 'The Deans of Exeter', *Transactions of the Devonshire Association*, lxxxvii (1955), 1-24.

Richardson, Malcolm, 'Henry V, the English Chancery and Chancery English', *Speculum*, lv (1980), 627-50.

Roskell, J.S., Clark, Linda, and Rawcliffe, Carole (eds.), *The History of Parliament: The Commons 1386–1421* (4 vols., Stroud, 1992).

Stamp, A.E., 'Legal Proofs of Age', English Historical Review, xxix (1914), 323-24.

Storey, R.L., *The End of the House of Lancaster* (2nd edn., Stroud, 1986).

Wedgwood, J.C., and Holt, A.D. (eds.), *History of Parliament: Biographies of the Members of the Commons House, 1439–1509* (London, 1936).

Wilkinson, Bertram, *The Mediaeval Council of Exeter* (Manchester, History of Exeter Research Group Monograph no. 4, 1931).

INDEX

Variants of personal and place names found in the edited texts have been given in brackets. Place names are in Devon, unless otherwise specified.

DEVON AND CORNWALL
RECORD SOCIETY PUBLICATIONS

The following New Series titles are obtainable from the Administrator, Devon and Cornwall Record Society, 7 The Close, Exeter EX1 1EZ

Unless otherwise indicated, prices are: £15.00 UK, £20.00 overseas (surface mail). All prices include p/p.

At joining, new members are offered volumes of the preceding 4 years at current subscription prices rather than the listed price.

Fully-paid members are offered a discount on volumes older than 5 years if the remaining stock exceeds 20: please enquire.

ISSN/ISBN 978-0-901853-

New Series

2   *Exeter in the Seventeenth Century: Tax and Rate Assessments 1602–1699*, ed. W G Hoskins, 1957 - **05 4**

4   *The Diocese of Exeter in 1821: Bishop Carey's Replies to Queries before Visitation*, vol. II Devon, ed. Michael Cook, 1960 - **07 0**

6   *The Exeter Assembly: Minutes of the Assemblies of the United Brethren of Devon and Cornwall 1691–1717*, as transcribed by the Reverend Isaac Gilling, ed. Allan Brockett, 1963 - **09 7**

12   *Plymouth Building Accounts of the 16th & 17th Centuries*, ed. Edwin Welch, 1967 - **14 3**

15   *Churchwardens' Accounts of Ashburton 1479–1580*, ed. Alison Hanham, 1970 - **01 1**

17§   *The Caption of Seisin of the Duchy of Cornwall 1377*, ed. P L Hull, 1971 - **03 8**

19   *A Calendar of Cornish Glebe Terriers 1673–1735*, ed. Richard Potts, 1974 - **19 4 £18.00**

20   *John Lydford's Book: the Fourteenth Century Formulary of the Archdeacon of Totnes*, ed. Dorothy M Owen, 1975 (with Historical Manuscripts Commission) - **011 440046 6**

Extra Series

    1   *Exeter Freemen 1266–1967*, edited by Margery M Rowe and Andrew M Jackson, 1973. *£18.00 UK, £23.00 overseas* - 18 6

Shelf list of the Society's Collections, revised June 1986. *£2.30 UK, £3.50 overseas.*
http://www.devon.gov.uk/library/locstudy/dcrs.html.

New Series out of print:
1 Devon Monastic Lands: Calendar of Particulars for Grants 1536-1558, ed. Youings, 1955; *3 The Diocese of Exeter in 1821: vol. I Cornwall*, ed. Cook, 1958; *5 The Cartulary of St Michael's Mount*, ed. Hull, 1962; *8 The Cartulary of Canonsleigh Abbey*, calendared & ed. London, 1965; *9 Benjamin Donn's Map of Devon 1765*. Intro. Ravenhill, 1965; *11 Devon Inventories of the 16th & 17th Centuries*, ed. Cash, 1966; *14 The Devonshire Lay Subsidy of 1332*, ed. Audrey M Erskine, 1969; 7, 10, 13, 16, 18 *The Register of Edmund Lacy, Bishop of Exeter 1420–1455* (five volumes), ed. Dunstan, 1963–1972

Extra Series out of print: Guide to the Parish and Non-Parochial Registers of Devon and Cornwall 1538–1837, compiled: Peskett, 1979 & supplement 1983